Preface

Revelation ...

Golf is not what you think. Golf is not what you try, either. It is not easy. It is not hard. You might be wondering: then what is it? This is a good and interesting question. To understand and know what golf *really* is, let's examine, discover and determine first, what it is not. By observing nature's perfect balance and harmony, we can see God has arranged a specific order to everything. This didn't happen by accident. It is not coincidental. Apparently, mankind's common assumption is that by his/her own thinking and trying, he/she can somehow manage to improve on the system. Rather than simply tuning in to the relaxation that comes by trusting in The Almighty, they can complicate matter by making themselves miserable through incessantly thinking and trying *harder*. We all might as well "knock it off"! It doesn't work that way. It never has; it never will. Stress is the result. After distinguishing this, the picture can clear. Two primary questions now need to be asked:

1. Can you imagine?
2. Do you believe?

If you are ready and willing to play along with me, I believe you'll become able to draw positive, meaningful conclusions— to not just help your game, but also, improve the quality of your life! There's a different game out there. I know because I found it. It doesn't involve ego or competition. You don't have to measure yourself against anyone else. You don't have to judge or be judged. You don't have to be unhappy or miserable. Thus, all it needs to take is a certainty (sureness) in surrendering to your Highest Authority. There is a joy in playing golf that many have never come to realize before. For those, it may seem like a vicious circle of frustration. As a former member of that establishment, I'm here to relate that, as intriguing as all the golf articles that have ever been described and shown through infinite illustrations and trials are, God keeps teaching me that there is an ease to be found in each and every one of us that can't be taught by pictures or words upon words. It's a realization of becoming content with who we are. We *all* belong as God's children. He loves each and every one of us. There are no exceptions. When we get off His path, the answers will not be there. This book is devoted to honoring Him by working to help others get back on track. God has shown me how simple it is. It is for you, too.

Table Of Contents

Introduction ix

Chapter I   Safety & Etiquette 11
Chapter II   Instilling Confidence / Building
                Your Swing 14
Chapter III   The Importance of Mechanics /
                Understanding Basic Physics 18
Chapter IV   Setting Your Boundaries / Knowing
                Your Rules 39
Chapter V   Selecting Equipment 44
Chapter VI   Scoring & Handicaps 50
Chapter VII   What Most Lessons Leave Out /
                The Search "Within" 55
Chapter VIII   I Don't Like / It's Too Hard / I Can't 62
Chapter IX   Goals & Dress Codes 65
Chapter X   Gambling & Competition
                (The "Macho" Addiction) 68
Chapter XI   Cheating & Electronic Dishonesty 72
Chapter XII   The Driving Range 75
Chapter XIII   Public Vs Private 79
Chapter XIV   Costs 82
                A. Personal (Commitment)
                B. Prices (Economic)
Chapter XV   Golf's Current Culture 85
Chapter XVI   Comedy / Drama 88
Conclusion   A Summary of What Golf Is 91

Inroduction

We may think we're in control but,
GOD IS IN COMMAND OF EVERYTHING.

Here's an example: Imagine...

I t's the fourth hole of the U.S. Open qualifying round. It's your initial try at this. You have parred the first three holes that are behind you now. Having that under your belt, you think you're on the verge of glory. You've practiced the course and reviewed your notes. You think you're prepared to tee off on the next (relatively short, dog leg to the left) par four. You recollect: during your warm-up play, you had used the driver to cut off the dog leg, but had shot too far through the fairway and out the other side into the rough. (Note: If you have ever seen or experienced U.S. Open rough before, you know it's not conducive to a high percentage follow-up shot). With all of this in mind, you decide to aim the same line as previously thought, choosing a three, or a four wood instead of the driver (which was the wrong club before). Oh, God! Which one? Think, think, *think*! You know you can draw a four wood a little more to accommodate the bend in the fairway. It seems like a good choice, so you hit it!

The flight's good; you caught the sweet spot; it's a perfect shot or so you thought... "Better load again." A voice pierces your concentration as you watch the ball land in horror a foot or two left of the white out of bounds stake. Where did that come from? You'd never seen that there before. You mutter, "What the hay?" as your heart sinks; your dream crushed. You finish the hole with a triple bogey, seven. You realize you're toast. You try to hang in there valiantly and end with seventy-nine score. You know you blew it. You say to yourself, "I tried so hard. Why did I fail? I thought I was good enough…" Well, let me be honest. That's what you got for *thinking*. You had it coming. Where was your *trust* in God—who was right there with you all along?

What does God have to do with it!? Everything! …and you thought you could do it alone. Okay, okay. That actually happened to me, but can you understand how I got in my own way? God gave me the gift of talent. Who still thinks that is enough? The truth is, only one tenth of one percent (one in a thousand) of all golfers, break 80 consistently for 18 holes. Maybe one in ten thousand of those will succeed on tour. Still want to try? Where most fail is that they don't trust enough. Now, I realize that if you're a newcomer to golf, or maybe haven't even begun, this story I've just related may seem a bit too involved. However, I must impress a point at this stage: that you have a distinct advantage in the fact that you have far less to undo than the experienced player who might be clueless.

Either way (and I apologize if I've offended any experienced players), remember that I include myself in this category. Been there, done that. What I have gained from starting anew various times is the knowledge and confidence to work to be your guide through the following chapters. However, don't just take my word for it. Trust God and search with "in", not with "out". I Love You. I'm here to serve.

Chapter I

Safety & Etiquette

"**I** Love You?!" Yes! That's why I'm concerned for your safety above all else. It must be top priority. Where do you see or hear the most important aspect of the game talked about anymore? Have you ever been hit by a golf ball or worse yet, hit somebody else? Fortunately, I've only come close in both instances. I've seen people badly hurt, even maimed (losing eyes and such) and know friends who have witnessed deaths at the hands of careless players. Golf is meant to be joyful for everybody (which, on a scale, is way higher than fun—a superficial substitute). Nobody needs to allow such selfishness and impatience to cause the avoidable breaches of safety. Spread the word to the head pro, the starter, your friends and playing partners that you will not tee off on any par three or four until the group ahead has not only cleared the green, but moved on to the next tee box. People are not cattle. There's no justification for "pushing".

Also, on par fives, wait for the group to be beyond 400 yards ahead (yes, some people can actually hit that far). If this seems too unreasonable, consider "crowding" most annoying and dangerous. Imagine you're playing in back of your own child. Now how do you feel about shooting prematurely? You don't prefer balls landing in *your* space, do you? Etiquette begins with this common courtesy. It is also known as the "Golden Rule". In its origin, golf was regarded as a "gentleman's" game. Why "gentlewomen" weren't mentioned, I can't answer. Nevertheless, these "gentle" assumptions have continually been eroding. When did these noble considerations begin to be ignored? Maybe it started with the first "tailgater." Violators used to be heavily fined for this rude and extremely hazardous offense. Now, being so commonplace, it's sometimes hard to find a motorist who doesn't.

Choose to be better than that! Fix ball marks, whether they were caused by you or not. Repair divots in the same manner. Pick up trash—just because it's the right thing to do. Lead by setting an example. If legacy matters to you (which it should), then your departure must be left in more pristine condition than when you arrived. In other words, "Clean up your mess." Thank you! Here's a "for instance": Imagine please (even if you're not), that I'm an average golfer that shoots 100 for 18 holes. Now figure in how many practice swings I took per shot. The median number is about three. Whoa! Ponder that for a minute or two. Now, consider adding 300 more swings to my score (putts count, too) and the grand total of 400 is perhaps why I feel drained when I get home, fumbling and grumbling to get to my easy chair, while my honey asks how my day went (if she hasn't left me by now).

Also, I reflect the course seemed to be playing slowly and how much my practicing technique affected others ("Hey! You bleepity, bleep, bleep, bleep...!"). Oh, they were referring to me?! Was I considerate? Uh... Realize that only one "perfect" swing can exist for each shot. Why waste it over a practice swing? Step up to the ball and at least look like you know what you're doing and fake it if you must. Hit it. Please, keep moving forward. It's so simple to do. One more consideration is this: Even a touring pro will admit that he/she only experiences approximately four "perfect" shots per round. I ask my students how often do they "try" for it? The common response is, "Every time." Really?! Miracles happen only on God's timetable. Disregard such foolish attempt by giving yourself plenty of margins for error. Accepting results less than exact will relieve pressure and allow room for improving at any level.

You'll be doing yourself a huge favor for starters. "Trying" to be "perfect" (which I used to do) is futile, resulting in ultimate disappointment. Most of us have had the dubious privilege of watching a foursome take an eternity (10+ minutes) to all finish putting the ball in the hole (but no, I'm not dedicating a chapter on how to line up a fourth putt). This type of bad play may be humorous to read about, but not play behind. So many try to copy what they observe. Like being nude, they are completely exposed when doing so. The pros do it on TV. They squat a lot, fuss about and stick their putters out. We're watching from the tee box amongst friends in our group and invariably at least one will call out, "Squatter!" and point. "Looks like they're reading a paper, taking a dump." "Hey Smails (referring to the judge in "Caddy Shack"), $100 you miss that putt!" We win a lot of money that way (figuratively, of course). A huge percentage regularly misses (even those pros). So... the point is? I observed a fellow just the other day, doing the "push it out" position on the practice green, on short putts and then he'd stand there miffed, wondering "how" or "why" he missed.

Really, even the experts on TV don't need to show off so ridiculously. They're mainly "milking" camera time. Plus, if they knew how silly and embarrassing it appeared, they probably wouldn't do it anymore and the commentators would feel less inclined to jabber. The solution is the same: pull the trigger already. It's either going in or it isn't... Take your 50/50 chance, because the odds don't improve the longer you look at it—but enough on that for now. More could be said about etiquette. Perhaps you can come up with some of your own examples to improve courtesy. The bottom line on this issue is to laugh about it a little, take it much less seriously and set the good tone instead. I promise you'll have more energy, more fun and play better in the long run.

Blessed Wishes

Chapter II

Instilling Confidence / Building Your Swing

Either you are confident or you're not. To test this theory—walk into the pro shop (the more witnesses, the better) and then say to the head pro, "I hear members tell they think you swing like a girl. Is that true?" What you've done is actually paid him a complement (girls have better, natural swings). Instead, you've most likely caught him "off guard" and "rattled his cage". If he's truly "worth his salt", he could come back with a witty reply. If this is the case, you've found a good one, willing to see you eye to eye. If he balks, or looks nervously away, you've spotted a phony. (Note: It's wise to have an "A" player for a friend to back you when you're doing this). Then go for, "How about we meet out on the course and give you a good whooping?" and add something like, "We haven't got your kind of money, but does $5 each per hole sound like enough? You play your 'straight-up' game and we'll play 'best ball'."

Now you know you're in his head, because he can't afford to look bad. If the head pro is a woman, game's off. Go pick on somebody your own size. You also could use a little more subtle approach (but confident nonetheless). Walk up to the counter (gender indifferent) and ask, "Did anybody turn in a Top Flite 3?" If they look puzzled (a distinct probability) and respond with, "What, a head cover?" Say, "No, my ball. I lost it somewhere on such and such hole. It's my favorite and I hoped someone was honest enough to turn it in." Pull this off by keeping a straight face and watch the reactions... You can laugh later. You might even delight in altering their day. After all, you just came to play a game. They're just there to take your money. Now, who do you suppose is the boss? Don't let them intimidate you just because they might have a "title". Also, please—beware of asking for lessons. Once again you're looking for help and they're looking for money. I'm here to help you to help yourself, but enough about my confidence, let's get going with yours...

When I start a class, whether it's beginners or not, I'll stage the same situation: "How many shots will it take you to make it into the first hole (as I point to #1, or ask them to visualize)?" The usual response is, "I don't know."

If someone offers up a number, I'll say, "Are you sure?" Any hesitation is what I look for. "Would you rather choose a simpler path to develop from?"

The unanimous choice has always been, "Yes!"

"Then, please come with me." We walk together to the practice green (or a flat, level, smooth surface, with plenty of space indoors). "Instead of starting at the tee and working toward the hole (which is more difficult, as well as much more laborious and confusing), who would prefer starting at the hole and "growing" toward the tee (which is much simpler by practical means)?" Affirmative answers abound. "Good!" It bears explaining that no great player has ever existed without becoming a great putter, first and foremost. Since putting is half the game, in and of itself, you should devote half your deliberation to this facet of the process. In other words, right choice. I like to assume nothing and by putting myself in your shoes, it helps me imagine what you're going through, just as I did (and still do) each and every time. I've just had a lot of practice, so, perhaps it's become more "automatic".

Returning to the physical experience, I place a ball on the ground roughly six feet from the hole (indoors, you can use a large coin or something approximate in size). "Who can make this shot every time?" No response, other than blank stares—whereupon I pick up the ball and move it closer to three feet. "How about from here?" A majority of shrugs persist. Still not convinced, I place the ball at one foot from the target. "I think I can probably do that."

"*Think*? That's not sure." To four inches it goes. "*Here?*"

"Well, I can do *that!*"

"Then, *here's* where we start!"

This shows that just as a child learns to walk by taking baby steps, confidence grows by establishing, and repeating success patterns. Tap the ball in with your toe, and then go get a putter. Congratulations, you've passed the first exam. Keeping it simple is the key to instilling confidence, so, always remember, "Wherever you're going or how far you get, there you are." —Anonymous

Here comes the BIG test and then we'll proceed. "Do you believe?" If you don't, you just did. That… you can "think" about. I believe, you're ready to build *your* swing. I mentioned in the Preface that golf isn't easy and it isn't hard. It is also not something you can rush to get. It requires patience, diligence and persistence. The character Red Green ("The Red Green Show" — PBS) might have put it best when he said, "We're all headed for that brick wall. Just how hard do you want to hit it?" I would like to take you now, step by step, through the process of teaching yourself, so that you'll never have to rely on somebody else to "try" for you and pay them to do it. Let's begin…

Hold the putter grip gently between your thumb and forefinger (loosely dangling). With the point of a tee in your opposite hand, tap the toe (front end) of the club face. It should release a twisting vibration of energy through your fingertips. The reverse effect can be felt doing the equivalent to the heel (back end). Next, from either end, tap your way to the center.

Do you notice the quivering decrease? When you have reached the true balance point, the club will pendulum softly to and fro. You have found the "sweet spot". Some club manufacturers claim their product widens the "sweet spot" area, but please— isn't dead center of the bulls eye a point size? Use a fine ink of some sort to mark this "exact" spot on the top of your putter, to see as this reference. If you happen to own a "precision" model, a line or an arrow may have already been etched on. Whichever the case, use this precise measurement to set this instrument "lined" to "dead center" and touching the back side of the ball while resting the "flange", which is the bottom of the club, flat on the ground surface. Place a ball four inches from the hole or target and make this connection.

If at any time, my wording confuses you, stop. Take your time. Begin when you're ready and if necessary, break it down more slowly. This isn't a race. Enjoy going your own pace. If you're in a hurry, this is not going to work. You might want to cut out some of the caffeine. Progression comes steadily, not quickly. Rushing the process destroys the proper tempo, which is most vital of all the mechanics. Cheer up; stay with me. We're right on track.

Chapter III

The Importance of Mechanics / Understanding Basic Physics

It was deliberate, that no instruction to "go" yet was given. All that's been established is a reference point. This is important in approaching each and every shot. Mechanics are imperative to build next, but are by no means, to be overly considered. I know a friend, who by all standards has virtually no mechanics worthy of trying to copy. After all, he's practically broken every bone in his body (including his neck) by playing world class rugby. However, being the "Master of his own technique," he applies what he can to how he does and by using a most positive mind set, accomplishes feats we could all envy. However, let's get back to the subject: mechanics.

Everyone needs a solid foundation to work from. It's our connection with the earth. The earth has basic laws (physics) that help explain how things are principally possible. As important as these are, they only make up approximately 10% of all golf's understanding. Most people who try golfing get stuck in this low percentage area, continually attempting to over-correct their swings. Cram-filling with gimmickry, excessive tips and other junk learning, instead of trusting and sticking with simpler matter, is a sure recipe for staying in the pits. Mechanics are certainly a challenging aspect to refine, as well as the most time consuming initially, but once you can grasp your own understanding of why it has definite measures, the universal relevance opens into an array of limitless and endless possibilities.

Let's begin with four primary parts of defining mechanics:

#1. Alignment
#2. Balance
#3. Tempo
#4. Follow Through

When working with students, I'll suggest spending ample time to familiarize themselves with their own style and to apply each of these segments in order. Devoting one week per segment is usually an adequate time frame. All of the four basics can be practiced using isometrics at home and "double-checked" using a full length mirror. Virtual application (handling of clubs), should first be a continuation of bodily maneuvers.

The good news is that four steps are the complete package you'll need to acquire and keep as your own knowledge. Let's get the ball rolling. When your car is out of alignment, it can't go straight down the road. Just as necessary as it is to "aim" your car, aligning with your target must come first. Call it, "Knowing where you're going." Not much can go wrong from four inches. Nonetheless, skipping this important step can lead to laziness, bad habits and faltering in routine procedures, which are essential to being a consistently good player. With the ball equidistant between you and your target, draw an imaginary straight line forward through the ball to the center of your destination. Lock in on a "speck" about three inches ahead of the ball, on that same line. This is the target line, which you'll need to know, when you're ready to set up your stance to it. Not yet... let go of any thought of whether or not there might be a curve. For starters, play everything straight ahead.

Practically all measuring in golf can be accomplished by knowing how to use perpendicular and parallel lines. Now, standing with your toe tips parallel to your target line, take a second ball in hand and move close to the object ball on the ground. Standing erect, tilt forward comfortably from the waist, until you're looking directly down at the object ball. With the ball in hand, drop it from the bridge of your nose and see if it freely strikes the ball on the ground. You may need to practice a few times, but be patient until you find that exact spot. You certainly don't have to putt from this position, but once you find it, wouldn't you agree it would be more consistently accurate?

Next, let's examine the alignment of your grip. Whether you're right, or left handed, or ambidextrous, you have a "lifeline" in each palm. You can easily find them by cupping your hands. The creases you see running up from the center of your wrists are those lines. Place them face to face on opposite sides of the putter's grip (this should look like you're "praying" upside down). You're free to slide either hand up or down, to adjust to your fit with one hand above or below (overlapped, under-lapped or interlocked), the other. It's your preference. I would recommend "tucking" your fingers underneath gently, while pointing both thumbs on a straight line downward.

There are no incorrect methods. Some advocate "wrist" putting, which allows the hands to flop backwards and for-ward. In this case, motion is generated with the forearms (from the elbows down). Many prefer the "locked" wrists approach, which involves using the upper arms (from the elbows up to the shoulders). If you are uncertain as to which to choose, give them both a chance to test for comfort. Whatever you end up deciding, using your "lifeline" to guide you ahead is most trustworthy. A common rumor heard too frequently in golf vernacular is, "Keep your head down." Something we all do as humans is look up from time to time (maybe it's in answer to a call). Hey, it happens; it's alright. "Keep your head down," holds no truth. In fact, it can be as detrimental as lifting your head up. Subconsciously, the brain can accept this term erroneously and cause the head to "drop" incorrectly.

I believe the accurate term to use is, "Keep your head still," or, "Balance steady." You can keep your head up or down. Just don't move it! Watch your head in a mirror some time, as you practice your "pendulum" balance. If you're familiar with a metronome (a musical time keeper), only one visible piece moves back and forth. If this instrument were inverted (turned upside down), can you imagine how it replicates the balance of the "path pattern"? Your head shouldn't be moving, either. Relax arms in to your sides, with your hands close in to your lap. Notice the face of the putter remains on a perpendicular plane to the target line, when swaying the wrists slightly to and fro. This will not readily occur if you choose to use an alternative grip (i.e. across the fingers), resulting in a "swinging door" effect (opening and shutting the club face), which can cause drastic inconsistency. Do what you like. I'm just saying…

Moving on, we place as many balls in a straight line that will fit putter's width apart, within six feet of distance from the hole or target. Align the putter between the first and second ball. Allow no back-swing in this exercise. For now, drop your "trailing" hand off the club and rest it at your side. Drag your leading hand to the hole and let the ball drop in or roll over the target. Repeat the same, between ball two and three. As long as you're successful, keep going, but as soon as you miss—stop! Back up the trolley. The purpose of this exercise is to prove how simply this can be "carried out" or rather, "carried in". After getting somewhat the "hang" of things, reapply the trailing hand, but realize its only purpose at this point is merely stabilization. It is not and should never be intended to steer or direct motion.

Please, don't attempt to go beyond six feet. Remember that continuing past your confidence range has not been prepared for. You are still too vulnerable. Albeit necessary to incorporate the other three mechanics, in order to develop the putting stroke, I wish to clarify and emphasize, that our current focus, is solely on the putting stroke, itself. Let me define that there are three shots in golf:

1. Rolling (generally this means putting), but different instruments, besides the putter, are possible to use for this effect.
2. Bouncing (commonly referred to as "chipping"), where, minimal "air time" and maximum roll are achieved.
3. Flying (known as "pitching"), where maximum "air time" and minimum roll, are used. Thus, a "drive" is actually a long pitch (in relative terms).

Putting is uniquely different than the other two, in that, a significantly alternative stance and grip are being used. Whereas "chipping" and "pitching" are performed by "swinging" through the ball, "putting" is done by "stroking" through the ball instead. Consequently, "putting" is more modified, compact and simpler, by degree of difficulty. It should always be considered as a safer alternative (percentage wise) to the other two shots, providing what the situation will allow.

"Balance" is the next ingredient we'll add to "alignment" here. Proper balance is achieved by "anchoring" your body in such a way as to not permit a gentle push to move you from your position. Therefore, if a stronger wind might be persisting, a more crouched, hunkered down stance would probably fit the occasion. Comfortable stability is the key. As for width of stance: very narrow (even feet together) for short putts and "tap ins". Only a shoulder wide (maximum) positioning for putts in excess of 40 feet, need be applied. Between five and 40-foot putts, an approach from approximately ten inches, to one foot apart, is sufficient.

Pendulum bottom is exactly six o'clock. Setting your stance directly even, so the ball lies in the middle, is concise. You may, however, prefer the ball "up" in your stance—closer to your front (nearest to the hole) foot. There is nothing wrong with this. It will permit you to catch the connection with the ball, on the "up stroke", giving it more "over spin" roll. Beware though; this will dramatically increase the chance of "stubbing" the ground prior to contact. It's that "law of physics" thing again. In case you're wondering if "dragging" the ball to the hole is "legal", there are no rules to practicing the feel of the stroke. A question frequently asked is, "How much back-swing should I use?" This is a great question! Nearly all amateurs (and even some experts too), use way too much. The answer is: the minimum to set up your "follow through". What's the minimum?

Imagine …

You're idling at a stop light. You're the first car and traffic is lined up behind you. The light turns green. Do you slam it in reverse to go forward? You'd better not. No, you squeeze the gas pedal and as the release of energy surges you forward, you continue acceleration to cruising speed when the next light in front of you turns yellow. Either you blast on through, or you stop. I would recommend stopping. The same principle applies when putting. Accurate distance measuring is not determined by how much back-swing to use, rather, how much follow through to give. Practice this: Place your putter directly in front of the ball, facing your target. With a deliberate amount of acceleration, shoot the club head forward to the target and stop at that point. Keep at it, until it becomes simple and effortless to cover the exact distance. Then, do the same thing through the ball. Lessening or increasing the amount of follow through will depend on the severity of the "slope" (uphill or downhill, respectively) and by the speed of the green's surface grain.

An efficient way to test this before play is to approach the practice green with three balls handy. Giving the first an underhanded toss, notice how closely it rolls up toward your intended target. It's sort of like sensitivity training for the day. If the first ball winds up close to where you chose, you're ready. Otherwise, use the next two to make adjustments. Go on from there, but don't "try". I can imagine, it might have never felt quite like *that* before. Back-swing can be an inch, or it could be as far as your back foot, but no further (or you'd be asking for trouble). Remember (even for the hundred-plus footers), accurate distance is determined by controlled acceleration; follow all the way through (releasing your trailing side to turn up to 90° facing forward) to complete the task of "getting it up there" if you need the extra oomph. By holding back the full extension, you may find yourself unable to finish the distance. However, please—don't "try" to hit the ball harder. Instead, follow through more. Let yourself go!

Do you realize that a golf ball weighs less than two ounces? For practical purposes, let's say, the average golfer's weight is 150 pounds. How hard do you think you have to hit it? That poor little defenseless thing must think you have murder on your mind when you "throttle" the grip, wind-up with all of your might and "chop" like you're splitting wood. How hard would you "try" to hit a Ping-Pong ball or, lighter yet, a bubble? Now, doesn't "muscling up" seem to be ridiculously foolish? It is! Most people don't see this perspective well, initially. For, if they did, we wouldn't be witnessing all the "flailing" that goes on. My goodness, that's hard to watch!

Now, I must touch on tempo for a while. You need to know that this element of mechanics is most crucial of all. Without good rhythm, the other three are useless. I would rather lose my focus on the other three than this one because I can still manage a decent day. However, without proper, smooth tempo, all else can go completely haywire. Tempo can come at various speeds. One day it can be "The Charleston", the next day, a slow waltz. Steady as she goes is the ticket. Also regard it as, "Dancing to the beat." Even if you don't dance literally, I'm sure you must let songs play through your mind. Imagine a favorite and snap your fingers to the beat. Now pretend it in slow motion. There, you should be able to start "feeling" it. Take it one step slower still and you've just about got it. "I can't go any slower."

"Yes, you can!" Remember, swings can only go too fast. It's impossible to go too slowly. See if you can without intentionally "holding back". On the beat of one, draw in an easy breath and see how far your hands have taken your back-swing. Can you control holding it to an inch? My guess is you've gone way beyond that. Can you stop at one foot? You won't be able to control a one-foot putt forward if you're drawn one foot backward. You'll have to "decelerate" your stroke (the very biggest "no-no" of all). Go slower and shorter: one second/one inch, then stop. Count "two" (sharply), letting the air out as the "pent-up" energy releases forward—propelling motion to your target. As a result, you should be experiencing a soft, slow, deliberately short count on one, then a pause, followed by a strong, forceful count on two, to exhaust the power surge needed ahead.

Practice this, starting with the four-inch distance and work your way along. Always return to your "confidence" level, when you *begin* to struggle. You can pick it up from there next time. A couple of correctable errors most players tend to make are in the "thinking" process. They "try" to "make" everything. The other common "flaw" is to "think" too much about the line and not focus enough, on the "speed" of the putt. Most "three-putting" (or worse) occurs, from poor distancing and not bad aligning. It's far less problematic to be a few feet to either side of the mark, than several feet short or long. Recall, once again, that a controlled follow through combined with the right pace (that rhythm/tempo, thing) will net much better results.

One more item of consideration: don't be afraid, to putt in "gimmes". Denying yourself this opportunity at the "simplest" shot, is actually "cheating" your confidence. Just make the stupid thing. *You're* the one in charge! Whether you're practicing ten footers, or 110 footers, imagine a foot wide perimeter for the ten footers, to aim within: two feet from twenty; etc. Within ten feet from a hundred feet away, is a *very* good shot. Also, always remember: you can never "force" a ball to go in. You must "allow" it to do that. I tell my ball it has a choice: "Either go and find the hole, or I'll find your replacement." Let the ball know you mean business. It really works!

Would you like to sharpen your putting skills even further? My friends and I like to play a game called, "Closest to." The object is to see who can play their ball up "closest to" the hole *without* it going in (going in loses). No "marking" is permitted and we always leave the pin in. Hitting the pin is considered "in" unless, your intention (which you must declare), is to use it to knock somebody, who's closer, further away, via a ricochet. "Smacking" another player's ball out of the way with your own, to get yours closer, is fair play. Once the game is announced, one shot per player, starting with furthest away, ends the game. The closest is the winner, and gets bragging rights ("Na-na-na-na-na-na," to the others). Great laughs …Kids, especially (which we still are), love it!

Before we move on to the next phase, "Chipping, "there is a post script to putting. Take a pitching wedge for example, or maybe a nine iron will do and step off the green, beyond the "fringe" (the next shortest cut of grass), into the thicker grass. We all have to experience this situation sooner or later, so let's tackle it. Now, place several balls (10-12), side by side, say six inches apart. Using the same putting grip and stroke, align your club's "blade" (the bottom edge) with the shortest hole to commence. Stand up to the ball the same (you're putting, not chipping) and notice that the "heel" of the club, lifts up off the ground. This is intentional. Double-check to make sure the "blade" is aligned perpendicularly, with the target line. No "hooding" (closing to the "pulled" side) or "opening" (aimed to the "pushed" side) of the club face should occur. In other words, always keep the club face squarely on line with your target. Now, notice that the "toe" of the club is the only contact point with the ground. This enables the club to pass through the ball with little or no "drag" (which can happen by "catching" and "snagging" the "blade" aka trying a chip shot). There's a right time and place for that shot. This isn't it.

Centering this toe point of the club, directly up to and even touching the middle of the ball (as long as the ball doesn't "shift"), is perfectly legal. Use the same tempo as putting. Note: the ball should literally "jump" the rough though just barely, settle onto the "green's" surface and roll toward the target. Longer shots may require a lower numbered iron to reduce effort just as a sand wedge or lob wedge works better for the most delicate distances. As you become more proficient, with practice you'll discover not to change your stroke, but merely change your club. This simple shot scares too many players. Guessing how to do it won't get it done. I know that with patience and believing you can, you will. Even finesse shots require boldness. How are you doing so far? Are you trusting (I hope), or are you "thinking" and "trying" too hard? Be honest with yourself. It's the only way to be. I'm glad to be your guide, but you have to do this for and by yourself.

As we prepare to stretch our understanding of the "chipping" principle, you will need a mirror to see and prove to your conscious awareness what will be exemplified next. An understanding of "pivot" is required to perform adequately, so please, check how these techniques apply. I won't make this difficult, but it will be detailed and simple to act. Take it as slowly as you need to for comprehension. It's not designed for "all at once." This is the one reference chapter of the book made for you to return to for a guidepost, as many times as necessary. I hope that's clear. Ready? Here we go...

Face any wall with a mirror, eye to eye. It is vital to observe your reflection in order to check your development. If you are right-handed, take one step forward with your right foot. Align it perpendicularly to the wall, with the "outside" (not the "inside") edge of this foot. Take a moment to notice your right knee shifts inward, slightly. The purpose of this is to "anchor" your dominant side. During a back-swing, your right knee should never move in reverse of this now "locked in" position. This may feel odd at first, only because it might be new and different from what you supposed, or experienced in the past. For the left-handed, follow the same procedure using your left foot forward instead. A "locked in" stance with the outer edge of your left foot should be perpendicular to the wall and your left knee turned slightly inward, as well.

Now, with the preponderance of weight (60% or so), on the foot placed forward, slide your head until your eye level balances over the same knee. You should feel a bit "tipped" to the side. This is correct. It's time to bring your opposite leg up, to even with your "anchor" foot and parallel the tips of your toes with the wall. With the tips of your toes the same distance to the wall, rotate the heel of this "front" foot inward to 45 degrees. This will permit your "open" knee and ankle to "hinge" freely, rather than putting undue "twisting" stress on the knee and "rolling over" pressure on the ankle. Your foot spacing should be within shoulder width apart to allow a full "pivot" (note: anything wider will prevent necessary balance transfer forward to complete the follow through process). With your leading foot lightly balanced and front side "hinged" openly, shift laterally, using your "anchor" side to shove forward along the target line. Can you feel your front side alleviated to receive the balance of weight transfer? That's precisely the way it should feel—effortless.

You also might notice that the surest way to maintain balance, is by staying proportionately on the "balls" of your feet, without being too far forward on your toes or too far backward on your heels, with knees flexed not bent. Before anxiety strikes to do this with a club in hands, "Hold your horses!" Stay with me—no "jumping the gun". I mentioned "pivot" before. Let's get to know its relevance. With your head positioned over your "trailing" side knee, you can see that your front shoulder is elevated slightly higher than the rear one. Now, imagine drawing a straight line, from the base of your "anchor" foot, upward through your leg, continuing past your hip, traveling diagonally across your upper body and exiting out of your front shoulder. This resembles the "axis" on which your swing will "pivot." Just as the earth revolves on its "axis" this is how your swing works best. To test this theory, make a fist with your dominant hand

and press it against your side, just above your "trailing" hip. This located muscle is the center of your "axis", from where energy is to be stored and released during the course of your eventual swing. Keeping your head in balance, push in your fist, while "pivoting" 90 degrees to face your target.

When you feel the need to "give", allow your "anchor" foot to release and rotate onto the "ball" of your foot, and then, all the way over onto the top of your toes, after your heel detaches from the ground. If you're accustomed to swinging "flat-footed", with your balance in the middle of your stance, you'll be trying to swing with just arms, as your lower body, remains mostly stationary. This inhibits the "flow" of energy and restricts projection. Doesn't this make good sense? Do you now feel the "freedom" to not be holding back? If so, let's add a little more "seasoning". It's time to bring "counterbalance" into focus. Turn your "leading" shoulder by "rounding" it in toward your chin. This will enable your arm to twist just enough to allow your elbow, to face directly toward your target—perfect!

Take a moment to reflect on stance. Just as in "putting", please give no consideration to bending from the knees. Slight "flexing" is preferred, whereas "stiffening" goes too far. Tilt forward, comfortably from the waist, just to the point where your arms dangle freely and can pass back and forth unrestricted in front of your body. Do not pass perpendicular with the ground surface. In simpler terms: no reaching! In baseball, the arms normally swing horizontally; in golf, vertically. I believe I left you "hanging". With your "leading" arm "dangling" vertically to your side, elbow facing target, make a somewhat relaxed fist and extend your arm straight outward, toward your imaginary target, leading with the outside edge of your fist (same motion as a turn signal). Continuing this exercise, let's add more to it to "simulate" your swing.

Returning to your starting position, this time with your "lead" arm hanging down, evenly with your "front" side, open your palm and extend your thumb toward the rear of your target line. We're about to connect your stronger arm, but we need to do this slowly and deliberately. With your "dominant" elbow "hugging" your hip, pretend that the two are connected. Bending up from this elbow, reach with this palm facing upward and attach your four fingers from underneath to the extended thumb of your "lead" arm. Notice the "V" pattern formed where your hands join. Reaffirming your head balance over your "trailing" knee, peek through the "V", the "point" of which should be aiming at your "front" knee, visible in the center. You are now "counterbalanced".

To complete the exercise, I'd wish you to adjust your tempo to "ultra" slow motion, in order to sense every movement along the way. You are about to experience, *your* "true" swing! To my knowledge, a car has yet to be built with a steering mechanism attached to the rear. I believe we can all chuckle at the idea of this. Why then, do so many golfers "try" to steer from the rear?" I suppose they "think" that their dominant strength should do everything. Well, that's just the thing… it's in the "following" position, not the "lead". In order to be in control of your swing, you must learn to let your "front" side show it the way. With your guiding elbow, initiate your move, very slowly toward the target, allowing every part of your body to follow except your head. When you've come to the point where your "trailing" arm is parallel with and aiming at your target straight ahead, rotate your head (keeping it balanced) and allow your arms to finish upward, releasing your elbows, to bend and collapse beyond complete extension.

Have you realized that during this maneuver, your dominant (trailing) arm was led into an "uppercut" position to complete the "thrust" of power, upward on a line, toward your target, rather than a wild "round-house" punch? If your "anchor" foot is still "attached" to the ground, shame on you. You're holding back. When you've completely released your follow-through, your balance of weight should be thoroughly transferred to your "front" foot. Only your rear toes should be touching, with the "trailing" knee now pointing at your target as well, alongside your "front" knee. Whew. Congratulations. You made it through a lot of commas. "How you like me now?"

Here's where we need to pause and reflect. "We haven't gotten to where we're going, but, thank goodness, we're no longer where we have been." I learned this principle from Joyce Meyer. She's great! Reigning in emotions is essential. Keep an "even keel" in perspective. Beware: on the balanced side of excitement awaits disappointment. Be in control of these dia-metrical feelings. "Chipping" is an abbreviated, variant swing. It should be considered when the putting stroke is no longer a feasible alternative.

Imagine...

You have a fairly wide opening to the green—you're, say, 50 yards short of its surface and the pin is placed at the far side... You *could* "smack" a putt of some sort and roll it there, but this might not seem to carry a high probability of success. You might be considering a "pitch" shot with a "lofted" club, like a "lob" wedge, sand iron, or "pitching" wedge, for instance. If this is the case, I'd be willing to expect your "lob" wedge shot to land short, in front; your sand iron might make it to the middle and your pitching wedge will likely go over the back of the green. I'm not saying they will; it's probable or likely. Instead, visualize a shot with a seven, eight or nine iron (depending on the "slope" and "speed" of the green) bouncing up to the front part, then rolling across the surface, up to the pin. This is much simpler to execute with confidence than by guessing where to land a pitch.

You must develop a vivid awareness of your own creativity, rather than allowing timidity, to limit yourself to one favorite shot in fear of all others. There's no need for that, my friend. Experiment and be bold! The world doesn't depend on your ability to avoid "screw-ups" from time to time. The less you are afraid, the more often you will be rewarded. That must be left up to you. In "chipping", we're going to abandon the "lifeline" grip that we use for putting only. With your "leading hand" open, lay the handle (grip) of the club perpendicularly across your fingertips. Gently wrap your hand around until your thumb is attached and pressing (as a push button) from the back-side of the grip, able to guide and move the club forward along the target line. If this feels foreign, consider this analogy: if you were to karate chop something, would you believe it to be more effective delivering the edge of a fist, or the backside of a hand? If you thought "hand" before (and this is actually taught a lot), can you picture the pain of your wrist breaking at impact? I know you don't want to… so, why anyone would want to hit a golf ball that way is beyond me.

Personally, I keep my wrists locked and deliver all my "chip" and "pitch" shots with the straight outer edges of both fists in unison. Collapsing the lead wrist at impact is disastrous to any shot. Applying your dominant hand to overlap, under-lap, or interlock will turn into a "power" grip if you align both thumbs in the same direction. Be careful, however, not to let "muscling up" become a tendency by gripping too tightly. This can produce "duck-hooking" and "over-steer". A gentler laying of the underneath thumb—relaxed more "overly" on top of the grip—is likely a better, more controllable option. As you experiment with "chipping", realize the sound of the word "chip, implies its own meaning, as well as the sensation. This swing should also be imparted in "two count" rhythm, as putting is. A whisper soft back-swing, pause and "chip," is the ball popping off the club face (like pushing sand out the door and off the porch with a broom).

Using a directive of the first count to start at six o'clock, back-swing to five o'clock for right handers; seven o' clock for left handers, and then pause. On the second beat (or the "chip" count), release the pendulum forward (to eight o' clock for right handers, four o' clock for left handers). Pay particular attention to detail, when setting up your stance with the ball's position, because "precision" needs to be addressed here. We're not "trying" for "perfection"; we're avoiding being "lackadaisical". Take your "anchor" foot and place the inside of your big toe pointing at the backside of the ball. Use a "prop" (a long club, like a "driver" will do) to familiarize yourself and help position your next step. Lay the "prop" on the ground, with the grip end placed evenly at the inside of your big toe and the "shaft" pointing at the ball. This should be perpendicular with the target line. Now, rotate your "anchor" heel outward, until the outside edge of your foot bisects the angle of the "prop" and the target line (45 degrees).

This is the most technical part to get through. Hang in there. The rest will be a "snap". With the heel of your "front" foot, place it flush on the opposite side of the "prop", with your toes angled open to 45 degrees as well and gradually slide it backwards (along), until both feet toe tips are at a 45-degree open split to your target line. This should result in knees closely spaced, in a very "narrow" stance, with "front" heel and "back" toe, respectively aligned perpendicularly to the target line. Now, your body alignment has been "compromised" in half. This is only recommended for "chipping" purposes and I'll explain why. This decreases the amount of energy needed to complete the follow through, by one half (45 degrees to finish turning, instead of 90). This means less effort, by using less movement, resulting in better control. This also enables a better peripheral look at the target (less turn to view). It does, however, require a concerted effort to keep your shoulders in parallel with the target. Failure to realize and do this can lead to backside "over-steering" that could radically cause problems. We don't want that.

If this posture makes you feel "ill at ease" you can resort to the "square" stance approach, knowing it's restrictions to "finesse". The difficulty most players have with the "chip" shot is either "skulling" (making contact with the "blade" edge striking the ball), or "chunking" (which is first "catching" or "snagging" the blade into the ground behind the ball). In consequence, many shots can be wasted. In response to the problems of "skulling" or "chunking," I would recommend the following solutions. Use the "open" stance approach. It may feel a little awkward to get accustomed to because it may be quite different from what you're used to, but it will certainly allow you to use more "finesse", which most definitely comes in handy in "tight" situations. Secondly, make sure to align the ball with your rear big toe, so that, with your hands being forward—even with your front knee—will enable contact with the ball at the "peak" of the downswing (hands *must* be leading the club through the ball).

The "edge" of your "blade" is designed to clear out the path in front of the ball, not what's behind it. Therefore, before you set up your stance, you should always align and set your club directly to the ball (no space in between), to let your body and brain know exactly where you intend to make contact first. After that, then, align your body. Do you understand the significance of "steady" balance, here? Keep your head still! "Chipping" is an area of the physical game that demands nearly as much attention as putting. It is probably where most number of shots can be saved or wasted. Therefore, it would behoove you to practice these shots much more than "tee" shots (which we'll get to). Some "green-side" sand bunkers can be negotiated using a "chip" shot and sometimes even a putter. Depending on the sand's texture, if it's hard packed or "crusty", you could "skim" the surface. If there's no ridge to stop it from rolling out, a putter is a great choice to use. If the ball needs a little "lift" to clear the top, "picking the ball clean" off the surface with an appropriate iron chip will do nicely. If the sand is soft and loose, "splashing" it out would work best.

The reason many shots fail to make it out of a trap is that the club head sometimes descends too deeply and gets stuck. "Sweep" it out like a broom's in your hands, rather than trying to "dig" it out like using a shovel. The follow through must accelerate to clear out the sand. As the sand is displaced, the ball comes loose with it. Sand will slow your club speed more than you might think. Be determined to pass through this obstacle with a "high-finish". When "splashing" is called for, the contact point needs to be determined at an inch (minimal) to two inches (maximum), behind the position of the ball. Contact between the sand and club is not technically allowed (by rule), before the actual shot is performed. Thus, this should be one of the rare moments when "waggling" the club head above the intended point of contact through the sand should occur.

Visualize the edge of your "blade" making a shallow (half inch to an inch) cut, before and below the ball. Keep the club accelerating all the way through to your target. Don't stop at the ball! A nice "spray" of sand flying should be accompanied with the ball. This is one of the most satisfying shots, when executed properly with relaxation and without fear. To avoid bogging you down with too much mechanical detail, I'm going to be brief describing "pitching". Picture an archer with bow drawn, aiming high into the air to drop an arrow at, or near an intended target. Does he/she "leak" energy "retracting" the string further or is the energy released by simply letting loose? To me, the answer is obvious. Remember the technique of placing your fist at the center of your axis and pushing laterally forward, as your pivot rotates toward the target? I hope so. Well, imagine that muscle is a "coil spring" that you wind-up like a watch. Winding too far breaks the spring and the energy is lost.

However, stretching a rubber band (to use another analogy) up to the maximum of "being taut" stores up energy to propel itself when it is let go! Therefore, drop the "open stance" used for "chipping" and tee up a ball. How "high" or "low" is your preference. It's important to know that whatever height you like to set your ball (I usually prefer a tall three inches), you must measure the "sweet spot" of the club you're about to swing to the center of the ball. If that requires the club being "lifted" off the ground to comply, so be it. I choose the "high" setting because I want a "clear runway" path for my swing, with little or no chance for ground interference along the way. If you want to experiment with any pitch shot on the playing field, you can "tee up" for everything (unless you're in a tournament). Who are you going to let tell you that you can't?

As for aligning a pitch shot, measure the ball evenly with the inside of your "front" heel for "tee" shots (to make contact at the start of your "up-swing"), the center of your stance for "level" shots or slightly "uphill" lies and the "back" foot—big toe, predominantly. Never "try" to "lift" the ball up. The club face is designed for that purpose and will do the job if you'll just "let it" work for you. When confronted with a severely uneven stance (uphill, downhill, or side hill), first consider whether you are willing to risk injury. If not, put your ball on "level" ground (once again, unless it's a tournament) and if questioned, tell them to "bug off". Otherwise, put your feet together to swing on a straight up and down axis. This makes pivoting on the spot simpler to execute (or, you'll wind up losing your balance, to the direction of the downward slope).

When perplexed by being in a fairway bunker, consider "flinging" it out with a rake (once more, unless the tournament thing). This gives the rake multi-purpose (prompting "tee-hees"), besides smoothing footprints. However, if you must, play the ball "back" in your stance, allowing two extra clubs to negotiate the distance you wish to achieve (so, if it's normally nine iron distance for you to the green, use a seven). Contact with the ball should come before the sand. Sand diminishes club head speed. That's why, use more club. Start with five yard shots to build confidence and work your way along, as described earlier in the chapter. We must not miss understanding the correlation between increasing tempo count and increasing swing measure. Since a "chip" swing decreases the energy of a "quarter" swing by one half (because of the 45 degree open stance), let's consider that to be an eighth of your complete swing. By using a "square" stance that closes the open one, the fact that you're producing twice the turn rate (now rotating 90 degrees) could double your distance (same two count rhythm); hence, a quarter swing.

Doubling that again increases your swing to a half. This means adding to the amount of back-swing leverage by two-fold (lead arm straight on parallel to four o'clock for righties, eight o'clock for lefties—keeping that "trailing" elbow "tucked in" and able to rotate around your hip side). You're going to need to add one more beat to the count. For right handers, "one" is to five o'clock, "two" is to four o'clock. Remember to pause. The count of "three" is the emphasis after the pause, to release the pendulum motion to complete its momentum to ten o'clock. For left handers, "one" is to seven o'clock, "two" is to eight o'clock, and then emphasize a pause; "three" finishes straight forward and fully extended to two o'clock.

Perhaps this is the best moment to reemphasize that at the precise instant your back-swing reaches its end, there is that pause (usually quite brief, but distinguishable, nonetheless), which many, many players fail to wait for. It is this tangible split second that allows the club to "fall" into motion, pulling the player, to go along with it. Thus, the club-head initiates the beginning of the downswing, while the player simply "takes the ride." Does this make it plainer that God says when, not you? He controls the correct timing. Haven't you noticed (if you've played before), that when *you* "try" to control the timing by "leaving too soon," the ball doesn't go where you want it to, does it? The *maximum* "controllable" swing is a three quarter arm circle, with four counts, four being the "release" beat after the pause. Right handers increase your "retraction" one more notch, to three o'clock—straight back, unbent and parallel, until your left shoulder touches your chin, *without* lifting it. Left handers go to nine o'clock (in the same fashion) and both complete the follow through, straight forward, until elbows bend, with hands finishing above, at twelve o'clock—thus possibly tripling your "output".

You can "choke" up or down (shortening or lengthening), how much "shaft" balance you wish. Note: as you increase club length, your pendulum will take longer (time) to fulfill. You must be patient and slow your tempo accordingly, to allow for this natural process. Rushing this upsets the timing. Now you have all these options at your disposal. Make your choices quickly, decisively and deliberately, from your wisdom of knowing—not from "thinking" and "trying". I realize this chapter was quite the booger. However, if you were unable to stay with the writing pace and digest it all in one swallow, that is not the point. Please use this chapter as a reference, to assist in answering your own "need to know" time frame. Mind you, it's only taken me all of my life—so far—and I'm still enjoying the learning! Remember to: "Feel the force; don't force the feel." —Bob Toski

You are on your way!

Chapter IV

Setting Your Boundaries / Knowing Your Rules

Very simply put, I don't like being around unhappy people. Noticeably, happy people don't join gangs or hang out in clubs. They don't gossip about other people's problems, while revealing most of theirs. "Whiners" are disconnected with their "Higher Source". I certainly don't want to golf with them anymore. I'd rather golf solo, surrounded by God's creatures stirring the air, than somebody complaining and making excuses. I say this knowingly and I understand the plight. I was formerly a worst offender. I have quite a strong sense of humor from growing up watching funny shows with my parents. Jackie Gleason, Carol Burnett, Sid Caesar, Flip Wilson and many others would fill our house with shared laughter on a regular basis. They have no peers today, unfortunately. Too much punishment, isolation and subjection to violence has made this a very unhappy world.

Being an only child offered no outlet for isolation or punishment. Thankfully, violence in our household was pretty much limited to Alfred Hitchcock, Sherlock Holmes and Perry Mason, for the most part, avoiding the graphic detail. Whereas, happiness is simply attained by living in harmony with The Creator (birds don't have breakdowns), strictness ruled over my life for a long, long time. That works well in the military, but

God wants us to enjoy life, not fight it! Learning self-discipline; now that's another story. I used to be very unhappy, but not anymore… Once upon a time, both an old friend I met in high school back in the 60s and I were introduced while "trying" out for the golf team. We matched a pair of 40's for nine holes that day and a bond formed. As fate would have it, we lived only a few blocks away from each other.

He wound up being number one for our school, while I alternated between three and four. He was a gifted natural, never having had any lessons. Not owning a pitching wedge or sand iron, I would enjoy watching him blow people away (including me), when he'd lay a nine iron practically flat to the ground and hit his "patented" cut shot, nearly straight up and down, landing it in or right next to the pin time and time again. He didn't even have to practice! He was the toughest guy to beat, due to his amazing creativity and even temperament. To this day, I believe with dedication, he'd have had a great career on *The Tour*. When I questioned him, "Why not?" he responded, "I don't like it that much." Wow! I, on the other hand, worked my rear end off. My first love was aspiring to play major league baseball (my natural gift), but discovered I also had golf talent mixed with a fierce, fiery temper and perfectionist complex (a bad combination) to go with it. I didn't know how anybody could "put up" with me and didn't care, when I'd get so angry and self-judgmental at my seemingly "poor" shots.

Depressingly, I didn't like myself much, either. At times, I would want to jump out of my own skin! This would wind up being my most difficult "handicap" to overcome, as I became stuck at two. However, I guess my friend had more faith in me than I did then, for it appeared that he was "saintly" in his tolerance of my tantrums. He would often tell me, "You need to get your head out." Then he'd add, "How long have you been playing this game?" while giving me "the look" (trying to at least induce me to smile). "Too damn long," I snarled and cursed with a scowl. I was so dense. Now, the interpretation of "getting your head out" could be taken a couple of ways. Most significantly, I believe it means something to the effect of, "Your *thinking* is interfering with your ability to play." I might have gotten that, but instead, I "thought" it was intended jokingly, as a reference to playing stupidly, with my head up my own behind (which was apparently true, also—and funny when you think about it).

Well, whatever, at that time, it didn't help settle my nerves and frustration. It definitely was *my* problem. Consequently, my head remained stuck for a long, long time. I just didn't get it. I know no one else has *ever* experienced anything like that before. Therefore, I only mention it to suggest probably 98% percent or more of all golfers display this affliction in various degrees. My hope is that by relating this "common" flaw, more will be able to identify this ridiculous reaction, to do something about it. **The Who** referred to it as, "Getting in tune to the straight and narrow." Yes, we *all* can! I remember many times being on the green, six feet or so from birdie, looking at my pal and thinking, I've got him this time. He might be 90 feet away and off the putting surface and chip it in. I don't have to tell you I made a lot of pars, do I?

The oddest thing was, he didn't appear to be comfortable playing from the "fairway." It must not have seemed challenging enough. I witnessed his first hole-in-one, on a 200 yard, par three, with a three iron. It was spectacular to watch it land, at the front of the green, roll across and disappear into the cup. I had observed thousands of male players from another friend's house on the other side of the street that ran parallel up the left flank of the hole when I was a kid, just getting interested. I never saw any shot come close to that one! He simply sashayed his way to the result of his accomplishment, while I felt excited and quite envious (more "handicap" to overcome). We each held certain advantages, albeit being very different in our approach. In the nearly 5,000 rounds we must have shared over 25 years or so, we're still just one shot apart, or maybe it's tied. Who can remember, let alone care? All that really matters is, "What's for supper?"

Whenever we would be paired with strangers (and this would occur frequently), if he were asked his score at the end of the first hole, his snappy response was, "Mind your own damn score!" This would create quite a sense of discomfort for them and me, as well. Whereas, I, you or they might have considered my friend to be rude in this retort, he couldn't be bothered. I came to realize the rudeness was actually in the question itself. "What did you get?" is imposing. That is in fact, the point of this chapter. Are you allowing somebody else to set their standards on you, or will you be firm in your own faith and convictions? Sometimes you have to, "Put your foot down!" —Dad

We would take these opportunities to fire up our "A" game. As a team, we were nearly invincible, consistently shooting in the higher 60s or lower 70s under these circumstances. The bottom line is: play according to your own boundaries. Make up your own rules, as long as you follow etiquette. Choose your playing companions wisely. Kick out "Grumpy" if you have to. If you cannot be comfortable with whom you're playing, just excuse yourself and walk away (I've had to do this in U.S. Open trials when the "cut-throat" atmosphere became too unbearable). Begin anew. There are plenty of nice people who would be delighted to share a game with you. I was recently asked if I would be participating in a group event. Ordinarily, I purposely avoid these, for evident reasons. My reply was, "Do I have to play like everybody else, or, can I play my own game?" After "huh" looks and negotiating terms, it was discussed and determined, that no controlled format was necessary and I could play freely. This was agreeable.

I hope this helps clarify that you do have choices here. When you learn to choose, like I did, to *allow* our "Heavenly Father" to be your playing partner (instead of *caving* to all the distractingly disruptive "outside" influences), He will guide you on that "straight and narrow" path (whether it's in the fairway or not). Remember, there are only 10 COMMANDMENTS to obey. If somebody whips out their "rulebook" to "try" to tell me, I can't "kneel on a towel," to keep my pants clean, I'll tell them, "Mind your own damn rules!" If you "believe", you already know what I'm talking about. If you don't, you'll find eventually yourself lost in the details. I formerly had doubts so, I did. Test this question: Are you better, or worse, after having played? Honestly (and I really *had* to battle), I was usually feeling worse and more addicted, until I faced up and realized, "It's NOT about *me!*" Then rules became simple and everything opened into a joyful journey. I have found faith was always inside me. I have faith in you, too. Do you have faith in yourself?

Chapter V

Selecting Equipment

Beware the advertisements! Now, I want to be careful, as not to insult any advertisers. I do, however, need to contradict falsehoods. Gimmickry has forever been a tool for selling worthless stuff. Remember "snake oil" salesmen and "swampland" offers? Thus, slogans like, "bigger sweet spot area" (it's a spot, for cripes' sake), "hits longer" (not if you duff it), "shoots straighter" (not if you hook or slice it), "feels softer" (not if you hit it on the toe or heel) are just a few examples. These claims may not exactly be lying, but are they fully truthful? I dare say they can influence regretful decisions. All I'm suggesting is don't let them fool you.

For instance, a very nice fellow came up to me and wanted my opinion regarding an instrument he'd just paid $100 for. He mentioned it was a "sale price" at well over 50% off. Its' shape looked like a driver, as he offered it to me for further inspection. I noticed it possessed a transparent, poly-something or other shell material, with an elaborate mechanism inside that appeared to be sort of a gyro-magnetic thingamajig contraption. "What the bleep is it?" I asked, scoffing, to which I added, "Forgive me. I'm not judging you. This... whatever it is, just looks so preposterous."

"It's designed to force you to know, when to open and close the club face," he said. I related to him that the process of what it's *intended* for happens as a natural occurrence related to pendulum balance and is not something that can be duplicated or replicated by any gizmo designed to perform an unnatural event in its place. It's that machine versus human element. After waggling it a few times, as it balked and twisted awkwardly, I handed it back. I was certain he had wasted his money. Do you remember "Iron Byron"? It was essentially a robot built to perform a swing, while measuring golf balls for distance and accuracy. I believe the "new" model will cost tens of thousands of dollars, but will enable the purchaser to stay home and never have to leave the couch. Of course, I'm being facetious, but I see things trending that way. After all, how many kids are inclined to go play outside rather than stare at an expensive *item*, twiddling their thumbs? Definitely, the scales are tipping in the wrong direction—*literally*! It's pretty sick, both mentally and physically, when you think about it. They get hypnotized.

I snicker to recall this guy who actually walked up to the tee, to join our threesome and pulled this fuzzy, goofy looking, animal head covering off a "waffle iron attached to a stick" that he only had to pay, $395 for (regular price: $649). It was the most monstrously outrageous club any of us had ever seen, that wasn't shaped like a sword for battle. The jokes came fast and furiously.

"Where do you plug it in?"

"I like my waffles with strawberries and whipped cream."

"Make mine blueberry."

"O.K. Let's find out; what you can do with it?"

He was very brave, taking our kidding in stride. We all stood aside and backed off respectfully, as we quietly watched three ungraceful practice swings go by. Eyes began rolling, as we checked each other's reactions. "Oh, brother" was silently mouthed about. Then it happened—he struck the ball with the most unorthodox lunge in the history of the game. The ball dribbled off into the rough, like a whimpering kicked puppy, as we all groaned painfully. Feigning his disgust directed at the ball, I blurted, "Don't blame it for running away like that. You hurt that little thing."

My friends all laughed, but his head drooped in dejection. Here was a soul in desperate need of some guidance and encouragement. I offered a pat on the shoulder. "Cheer up, old chum," I said. "You can't stay down with us." My friends were as patient as possible. I knew that for the next nine holes, my purpose would be put to the ultimate challenge. I use this example because, honestly, I'm not able to come up with a better one. He, being our guest, initially teed off first. Subsequently (the rest of the holes), the order was determined by age seniority (not by previous score). Consequently, being the junior/senior of the bunch, I would always go last. When it came up my turn, I approached "the struggler" handed him my driver and asked, "How much do you think this club cost?"

His guess was, "I have no idea."

My reply, "Five dollars for the titanium head my wife found in a bargain barrel, at a golf shop; 15 dollars for the custom 50-inch, "rifle 6.5" extra stiff steel shaft and ten dollars for the arthritic type grip (I don't have arthritis, it just feels great) plus the labor to put them all together and made to order for a total of about 50 bucks," was received with astonishment (perhaps from the length of my sentence). His jaw dropped when, without practice swinging, I sailed one effortlessly up the middle, with great distance. I'm not intending to be or sound braggadocio. I consider us all to be on equal terms. I do express my need to be helpful, by stressing points to get messages across. I stand six feet and one inch tall and it once seemed like all "standard" clubs (one size fits all) were pre-assembled, assuming (I suppose) that everybody was five feet, eight and a half inches. I eventually resolved that the player should not have to adjust to the club; rather the club needs to be fitted to the player.

I made this discovery, during U.S. Open qualifying, when I was taking a distance beating by these dudes who were five inches shorter than me that were thumping their drives consistently in the 280s (long for that era!), while I was playing my little 43-44 inch "Power-Bilt" driver consistently at 250. When I tried to "step on it", I would find myself constantly "pushing" or "pulling" the ball into the rough. As a result, this was getting my dander up. I failed to qualify (so did they), but I found my resolution. All this while, I felt "stooped," to reach my club to the ground. I was playing with toys. I needed to build weapons! I realized I had to add leverage to take the strain off my back and match my height. The day after, I took my entire set to the local golf repair shop and requested they put six inch extensions into every club. Everyone there looked at me in disbelief.

"You want what? I'm not sure that would even be legal to add that much," the guy behind the counter replied.

"I don't either, but I don't give a rat's patootie, anymore. I need some real clubs; not just these little trick toys. Let the *Golf Police* come get me."

"You got it," he snickered.

When they were completed in a couple of days, I was so thrilled (the anticipation had been almost killing me). I rushed to the driving range (where I'd taught) and just had to test my number one wood immediately. As I took it out of the bag, I reflected on how far my longest shot had been with it before. I managed to hit one a third of the way up from the bottom of the net that marked the end barrier, of the range. As I rocked the club back and forth to its new rhythm, I subconsciously memorized the much slower pace. I calmed my breathing pattern, as time felt to decrease. I placed a ball on a tee, as high as it would stand. I needed to back away from the target line a few inches, although now I could stand much more upright. A whole new confidence overtook me, as I knew the moment of truth had arrived. When I drew the club back, it felt as though it was a fishing pole with a much heavier lure attached. I patiently waited for it to pass its clearing stages, until it reached the peak of how far I could stretch with it.

That moment where the energy pauses was my trigger signal to carry it through into flight. When the club-head dropped with the big "whooshing" sound of a great bird in swoop, the club-face picked up the ball and launched it high—up towards the sky. When I arrived at the twelve o'clock point of my follow through, I turned my head and watched, as the trajectory of the ball continued to climb. When it reached the apex, it had long since cleared the fence. Touchdown came perhaps 30 yards beyond. I had cranked it well over 300 yards, on the fly! "Come back here, you bastards! I wanna kick your asses. Outdrive *me*, will you?" I exalted, mockingly. Oh, I almost forgot to mention... straight as an arrow, too—and on the very first swing! Well, I had time to write in about the time "Mr. Waffle Head" (adorably speaking) finally finished the first hole. We all ended up having a jocular experience, with lots of ballyhooing going on. He picked up extremely well on the joy we were all having together and decided to scrap the notion that more expensive gear, makes for better play. I suppose, "If you can't beat 'em, baffle 'em with b.s."

I began golfing at around age ten, when a neighbor friend of my parents, who I called "Uncle Joe," gave me his old, rather worn set of hand-me-down, wooden shafted, "brassies" and "niblicks" of sorts. They served me until they all ended up broken in the trash heap, along with many more abused clubs to follow, as I failed to see the blame in the "owner/operator". Did I mention before that I was dense? I had an immense amount of growing up to do. Anyway, a decent set of 14 clubs (brand new), used to cost somewhere between 150 and 500 dollars. "Top of the line" was mostly less than a thousand. The "sweetest" set I ever had were the "Power-Bilt" persimmon woods, with "Haig Ultra-Dyne II" irons. The sensation of teeing up a brand new "Titleist 100" and smacking it on the "dot" can never again be matched, by the "tink" of any metal head. It's like comparing an ash bat to aluminum. However, technology marches on.

Choosing the right putter is finding that unique instrument that matches your style. I've been using a double-bladed "Bulls Eye" for many, many years. Next to my wife, it's my distant, second best friend. I putt, both from the right and left side (depending on comfort with the "break"). The club has a concise, yet simple design. It feels *just right* to me. The *"just right"* one is out there for you, too. In 1977, I was 27 years old. I had nearly progressed to professionalism, so I knew it was time for some great equipment. Instead of trusting my own judgment, I initially sought advice from other professionals. I got an earful of, "You don't want these," and, "You should get those," until my head was ready to explode. When I came across the "Power-Bilts" and "Ultra-Dyne II's", I would be criticized for my "poor" selection. I searched on, being told, "These Hogan's are the best. They're what I use;" another would declare, "Where you want to go, only 'Titleist's' will get you there." There was no doubt as to their quality, they just didn't *suit me*. The more I was confounded, the more I was convinced to return to the ones that attracted me in the first place.

Much to the chagrin of the salesperson, I chose *my* favorites, for a much lower price than the aforementioned. I think I posed a threat, challenging their insistent persuasions. "You'll be sorry, you've bought inferior tools, but you can come back and trade them in for an upgrade. Of course, they'll be worth much less after you use them," he said, as I paid for what I wanted. "Thanks," I replied, while thinking, *I wouldn't recommend him for a promotion!* I'm surely glad I disregarded taking any of the "mumbo-jumbo" to heart. My "inferior" tools enabled me to fire a 62 at Rifle Creek in Rifle, Colorado. "Not too awfully shabby." —Jacinto Iniguez (a dearest friend)

Trust *your* instincts! My wife found a beautiful set of ladies' graphite shafts, including new bag, new head covers and a new pull-cart for $80, once used, at a yard sale. If you elect to be frugal, you'll do quite well...

Chapter VI

Scoring and Handicaps

Have you ever examined the *Guinness Book of World Records*? You'll find a preponderance of relatively worthless achievements. Goals such as, "Most consecutive bounces on a pogo stick", "Cups of coffee slurped in a week", "Number of hot dogs consumed in an hour", "Golf rounds played in a year", etcetera, etcetera, have virtually no meaning in the grand scheme of things. They are mainly ridiculous in nature or death defying in risk (jumping buses on motorcycles comes to mind, for one). The obvious conclusion is people will do anything to satisfy a need to feel import instead of just simply knowing their magnificent uniqueness. What seems to be missed by the senselessness of many of these feats is the realization that each person is already a one-of-a-kind masterpiece according to, and in the eyes of, God. The credit for anything is His glory, not any individual's. You don't have to believe me, but how proud would you feel to be crowned for having the most pimples on your face for all time?

You can shoot the greatest round of your life or the worst and I dare you to take your scorecard to the bank and ask, "How much will you give me for this?" Come on; I dare you. Scoring is one of the best ways to louse up your day. Trust this former "sour puss" on this one. I used to let the carry over effect spoil day after day, over such trivial nonsense. It's value is nothing, while likely costing at least some aggravation, exasperation, humiliation, perspiration, palpitation, persecution, shock, grief, whining, perjury, or even a heart attack, stroke and in cases of oblivion, money! Scoring is not rational or significant in any sense. Your grand kids aren't going to save your scorecards when you're gone. Maybe you want to compare your score with somebody else's. Perhaps this gives you some sense of perverse superiority, if your score is lower than theirs. Well, suppose the other person just rescued a family from a burning house. How heroic would that make you feel?

Imagine…

Scoring is the main, vain purpose behind virtually everything. "I'm faster", "I'm better", "I'm bigger", "I'm stronger", "I'm smarter", "I got more points" and on and on—these are symptoms of this corrupt practice. Thinking score mattered, importantly, was absolutely, by far, my most egregious "hang-up" (synonym: "handicap") ever! It constantly was my anger core, my temptation to cheat, the controlling factor of my drive to win (my primary cause) and the center/selfishness of my thoughts. Of course, I was obsessed. It made me crazy. Is it any wonder why addiction begins with that first "hit"? How many of you are still addicted to keeping score? It can take a long time to reach the point of enough. Now you know how you can save yourself the trouble.

I shoot recreational pool on Tuesday nights. A group of us gather at a friend's house and we play until ten p.m. For last year's Christmas get together, I brought greeting cards, plus a small gift for each. Inside every card, I wrote exactly the same message. It said, "Thank you, for being my *favorite* pool partner." If you're catching the riddle, you're noticing that all of them are my "favorite" (co-favorites). It doesn't make any difference who wins or who doesn't, who plays well or who doesn't. We respect each other; we care about one another; we have joy; we laugh; we encourage; we tease (but not to be offensive); *we play*. When we break company, we eagerly anticipate renewing our rotating partnerships the next time. None of us smoke, drink (alcohol) or *keep score*!

You should know, as well as I, that there *really* are no winners or losers—just participants. Champions are a fleeting thing of the past. God has everything recorded anyway. You can't fool anyone but yourself. My father taught me, "It isn't whether you win or lose, it's how you play the game." Are there seriously any doubters to this philosophy? If so, keep writing down those scores. You might find the sympathy you're seeking, but as "Major Payne" (Damon Wayans) put it, "Look in the dictionary between shit and syphilis. That's where you'll find sympathy." People aren't handicapped. People are challenged. Handicapping is a scoring system that only serves to promote cheating. Moreover, it's only cheating if you're keeping score. The best way to repent of this sin is stop *keeping score*! Let others, if they must. You don't have to. If this statement riles you, go look in the mirror eye to eye. When you're being honest, you know you need to get over it. Do you actually think young children at play worry about scoring? Where do they learn from? If they *do* know about, haven't you ever had to break them up for arguing? Bdbdbdbdbd…

I once knew somebody who joined the men's club I played in, back in the 70s. He established a 14 handicap, although I believe the only thing "wrong" with him in this instance was that he liked cheating to win. He'd play in tournament events, shoot in the mid-seventies and collect most of the "first-flight" hardware at the awards ceremonies. Most of the hundred plus members didn't like him and talked behind his back. Hey, it's what "clubs" do (and a main reason why "Homey don't play dat!" —Damon Wayans. At least… not anymore, I don't). One day, he bounced a check (okay, two "wrongs") for his dues. Well, he was kind of… kicked out of the club. However, I must confess I had a cheating problem in the past, too. Haven't we all? Did I mention before that I had an immense amount of growing up to do? Haven't we all?

If you are familiar with my favorite golf movie of all time, *The Legend of Bagger Vance*, the scene near the end, where "Junuh" decides that playing honestly is the only way to play, serves as a most inspirational role model to emulate. I have another example to make by comparison. A particularly disturbing case was of a fictitious ten handicapper, who somehow, miraculously found a possible way to shoot a scratch score of 68 during a competition that he promoted! This isn't "sandbagging"; this is "dirt-bagging." With a net score of 58, he must have been pretty proud of himself for cleaning up at his own event. Gee, there's nothing remotely suspicious there! Just a whole bunch of "red flags" and hearing comments, "That dirty, rotten so-and-so..." Course par is an entirely fair system to measure by when you play even-up and drop the incessant "handicapping" method. It will also save a lot of unnecessary computer wear and tear ("Oh, dear... what will we do?"). *The course itself is the challenge.* It's not something you can ever win at. "You can only play the game" (wisely spoken by many).

On the other hand, if you remained entranced by the endless calculation of meaningless figures, I guess you can "stare at a screen" a while longer... If timidity, shyness, or plain old fear is a difficulty, I have a humorous tale to tell. Some of the ladies were having one of their cliquish "pow-wows," in the parking lot after a round. One of the gals, who formerly worked in the pro-shop (a lovely lady, with mild mannerisms), was fixed on the score-card, while a heated argument was brewing over who got what. Overhearing this spat going on (and escalating) I approached their golf carts with a grin and inquired, "Whatcha doin?"

"Oh, we're just trying to figure out our scores."

Now, I realized I was risking danger, breaking in on a "cat fight", but this was just too good an opportunity to resist. "So," I said, "Is it worth all the fussing and fighting over? Why are you keeping score in the first place?"

They all stopped, with dumbfounded staring and my friend replied, "She makes us," referring to the president of the women's club and town mayor (not that it's relevant, but it might be).

"Really?! Well, why don't you tear up the stupid scorecard, go have a nice lunch and make each other laugh instead of cry?" I suggested they play that way from then on. I could tell the wheels were spinning as I tipped my hat and left.

I've resigned from competition for about two decades. I have more than a fair share of trophies and gatherings, over the years. All they do now is collect dust. Maybe, I should take them to the bank and... Never mind.

I know I'm one of *all* God's children and he loves me. This is all the reassurance I need in this world. I wouldn't trade my joyful play and service for trying to prove nothing, or anything at all...

Chapter VII

What Most Lessons Leave Out /
The Search "Within"

O nce, when I was in Tucson, Arizona, I watched from a safe distance as a middle-aged man was "trying" his best at a golf lesson. He was attentively involved in the instruction, being given by a much younger "professional". The older man was hanging on the instructor's every word and display of motion. As the student stabbed and plodded along, I noticed the teacher would check his watch and yawn frequently—obviously trying to hide the fact that he was bored. I felt my temperature rising as I was tempted to reveal his despicable insincerity. I figured karma would catch up with him and justify his uncaring misdemeanor. It was not my battle to fight. Similar to this student, I suppose, I spent a lot of time and money searching for answers and approval.

From the moment we're born, the first person we look to for this help is Mom. Then, if we are fortunate, Dad steps into the picture immediately thereafter. Our impressions are formed, mostly by one or the other, or both, during the early years of our development. You probably know this, but maybe have not been reminded of this influence in a while. That is why I'm bringing it up. There is a manner of learning order that pertains relevantly to the topic of which I would like to direct your attention.

Whether we are subjected to early reinforcement (and hopefully not discouragement), our characters are already being shaped, regardless of realization. We're much too young to understand and therefore, extremely vulnerable in our dependency. We have virtually no other option than initially having to trust people, for our needs. When these needs are not met or at best unfulfilled, chances are that in order to express these deficiencies, we display our displeasure and frustrations through crying, fits or both. This is normal reactionary behavior.

If we carry this weight from those early susceptible years to our first day of school, deep seeded problems may occur that teachers, most likely, are unprepared to address. Once this process has started, it can "snowball" into adulthood and wreak havoc. One of my favorite jokes goes something like this: Two young boys were walking home from Sunday school after hearing a strong sermon about the devil. One boy turns to the other and asks, "So, what do you think of all that Satan stuff?" The second boy replies, "I don't know, but if it turns out anything like Santa Claus did, it's probably just your dad." On the surface (which jokes are), this is hilarious. If you experienced confusion asking questions about religion (like I did), perhaps the answers you were seeking were just as elusive as these boys exemplify.

I learned that asking my dad, "Why?" would be deflected by, "Because, I said so!" Further inquisition would be met with a stern warning, or worse. I can imagine, many of you, have been there. Consequently, I didn't know "how" I was supposed to believe. I loved my dad and mom very much, although I feared my dad for a long time. He was a devout Roman Catholic his whole life. I went with him to mass services to "try" to learn "how". He would recite in Latin; I didn't understand, but I would stand up, sit down or kneel, when everybody else did. I didn't exactly feel reverent acting like a copycat. Trying to be like the others made no sense to me. Since I was allowed a choice of whom to worship with (not a bad thing), I found the alternative to go with Mom and the Presbyterians, to see what they knew.

The minister seemed kind and wise. I liked him. However, the messages felt like they were directed to and more suited for the adults. Socializing after service, I remember being scolded for putting too much cream and sugar in my tea. People congregated in their little areas of favoritism, discussing whatever they didn't like about someone in another group gossiping about them and carrying on small talk. I would always just want to get out of there. I couldn't wait to get home and into play clothes. I was much more at ease—and felt safer, more protected—in my own little world, even if it meant being alone (I'm sure you must be getting the irony here).

I regarded Sundays as "practice sessions," in "make believe". It seemed to be disingenuous and pretending—going through the motions. I craved *true meaning* and *real, purposeful* answers. I was seeking a personal relationship, with a direct connection (if there was one). I came to realize, eventually, that I was having one *all* the time. Each and every one of us has the ability. A common assumption is that we must be able to see to believe. Contrarily, the opposite is the truth. The "enemy" uses confusion to "try" to trick us this way. Just don't be fooled. As I continued to struggle in my golf endeavors, people would often tell me I needed lessons. Reluctantly, I obliged from time to time, until a major turning point in my life occurred. At age 28, I'd been working nights full time for a good many years at a grocery chain, so I could pursue golf during the daytime. I became anemic and contracted hepatitis, which tried to kill me. Determined this was not to be my end, I realized I had an important decision to make. I was going to have to give up my job or golf. My job earned good money, but my health and enjoyment were of much greater value. I had to get off the "merry-go-round".

I chose to take my savings and during my vacation time, I invested in pursuing the best lessons I could purchase and "go for it". At that time, Bob Toski was thought to be one of the best instructors in the world. I considered him *the* best. I sought his advice. I had become stuck as a two handicapper, so my average scores were about 74 (good, but not good enough). "For any of you who are not familiar with this man, he won the "World Series of Golf" in 1954, when that tournament was a premier event—regarded as prestigious, amongst the experts. They called him "Mouse", due to his diminutive size."(Please read ***The Touch System for Better Golf*** by Bob Toski). He was in his 60s when we met, probably 5'5" (stretching) and 125 pounds (with weights around his ankles and soaking wet). He possessed a mighty swing that was smooth as silk and thunderous in energy. The ease with which he delivered each shot was amazingly graceful and awe-inspiring. He had the magnetism of watching David beating up on Goliath.

I was awaiting my turn with him at the driving range, when he approached, greeting me with a warm handshake as we exchanged smiles. Then, he sat down saying, "O.K., Phil, show me what you've got." I was a bit nervous (being in the midst of greatness), but composed and confident enough to send a drive straight ahead, around 250 or so. He had me, "Stop right there!" As I screeched to a halt, he asked, "How many instructors have you had?" I froze in pensive thought. As I "tried" counting them up, he commented, "Never mind… obviously, too many!" He paused, briefly, as he gathered a boatload of information, from my *one* swing! He continued, "I'm amazed that you've somehow managed to coordinate and copy so many different techniques. I see numerous personalities you're exhibiting, but where is your swing? I don't see *your* swing."

Dumbstruck by his profound observation, I managed to mutter, "Can you help me?"

"You'll need to start over." He seemed genuinely a little "ticked" that I'd subjected myself to so much "quick fix" learning. "I mean literally forget all that crap and start over," he reemphasized.

"Sure," I sheepishly responded.

Soon thereafter, he mentioned to the entire class, that Jack Nicklaus had approached him once, seeking a "tip". Mr. Toski's reply was, "I don't give tips."

Can you imagine?

At any rate, I chose to trust this man and his team (which included Peter Kostis, Dick Aultman and Hank Johnson), because I had faith that my best interest was involved. This is vital, since it's very easy to be misled by those with ulterior motives. I had one of the best times of my life! For the next year, I spent the majority of my days honing my new skills with the help of visual reflection and "prop" reminders. I was delighted at becoming "the master of my own technique". Oh, I developed a great swing, alright. My biggest trouble (turned out later), was I still didn't know "how to play the game". Let me just say, for the next 27 years, or so, as it related to golf, I held my own. In 1991 (two years after my dad passed away), I'd had enough of city life and competition. My father loved watching me play ball, until he got too sick to attend games. It was time to move on. I said goodbye to former teammates and left for a fresh beginning, as well as to take care of Mom through her twilight years.

We moved to a town where I bought a house next door to my future bride. I quit smoking and made new friends, including a retired minister named John, whom I chose to baptize me on The Grand Mesa in Ward Lake. Things were going well. I liked my life, but, I still didn't like my golf game. I carried with me the same old issues that always came back to haunt and challenge my greater moments. I slipped into a funk. I was shooting in the high 70s and low 80s with my new buddies. I wasn't putting anything together and I wasn't happy about it. Then, one day out of the blue, all the pieces meshed while my mom witnessed my shooting the course record. She would pass two years after this event. I was so glad to have her with me. She delighted in driving the cart. As great as that miraculous day felt, two weeks later, I flung my entire set of clubs, bag and shoes into the reservoir, one by one. For a year and a half, I was done. I refused to be bothered until my ol' high school buddy looked me up. His unwavering proposal, to show up and give me a game (whether I had to rent clubs or whatever), lit my fire.

Now I could blame him (yeah, right). Within a year, my mother was gone. Alzheimer's had drained the life out of her and now, I was in need of revival. I recommitted and married my dear lady neighbor, who came to my rescue when Mom died. Four years later, we moved again. This is where and when, I met my golf "soul mate," who became the second person (after my wife), to help me untie the knot in my brain. I still had a long way to go in discovering "the search within", but as I stated, in the beginning, by first determining "what it is not". Well, I learned—it's *not* about me! I went through an *enormous* perspective change (which I had to be agreeable to welcome); plus, I needed to learn how to disallow the negative influences to enter by recognizing the culprit. All along I had "thought" it *was me*!

When I reached my 60th year, I made a horribly poor decision (unrelated to golf), that sent me spiraling into a nervous breakdown. Without elaborating on the details, I'll conclude, that I tried to control my life seeking solutions on the outside— to the point of self-overbearing stress. This life threatening health issue became the ultimate "awakening" that led me to "The God Source" within. When I was voluntarily admitted to join a society of down-trodden, beaten to the depths of hell spirits that were as close to death despair as a single breath, my soul was alerted to the righteousness I craved all along. The crucial moment had arrived to turn aside (lest be consumed by) every negative, outside influence "trying" to overtake me. I had to "cast the devil" to be "born anew" to the goodness that only God creates in all of us on the inside. It had been there, all the time, but I didn't understand "how" to connect with it until I surrendered the *fight* with my selfish ambitions, to totally commit the rest of my life to service that would advance His Kingdom. Eureka!

Thankfulness, gratitude, humility, honor and repentance are a few of the constant supplements to my daily spiritual diet. I didn't find religion. At the bottom of my self-inflicted desperation and solitude, I was "lifted up" to a brand new awareness of my very own personal relationship, with my God and Savior. The ascension was simple. All that is essential to bring is complete dedication and trust. I have not been happier, fuller of joy and contentment—ever! "Nobody can steal your joy. You have to give it away." —Joyce Meyer; Joel Osteen (and perhaps many others)

I'm not letting that happen anymore. Neither should you. The human element in all of us is so short-sighted and narrow-minded. What I mean to illuminate here is the fact that we're all continuously seeking answers to our dilemmas, but those conclusions are only resolved when we turn inward and acknowledge God directing us. Those who display conscience and goodwill toward others are aware of this universal law. "Doubters" and "deniers" are just "turned away", living on the outside. Faith is not something to be found on the outside, or through other people, or even in church. The truth remains on the "inside". It might be called, "The Holy Spirit" or "The Soul." It's the quiet knowing, that trust (faith), will lead us on the path of righteousness. "Though I walk through the valley of the shadow of death, I will fear no evil, for Thou art with me," (Psalm 23:4).

Each of our great individual destinations is awaiting us out there on *that* path. No amount of "thinking" or "trying" can ever replace or substitute the faith (trust) it takes to overcome *all* obstacles.

That *is* the lesson, my friends.

Chapter VIII

I Don't Like / It's Too Hard / I Can't

Simply put, when a person says, "I can't" do something; they are proclaiming that they won't, whatever it is. Of course they *can*, or at least God can, even if they won't allow themselves to. "I don't like" and "it's too hard" are pathetic, whiny excuses for a lazy way out. Keeping quiet would be a much better option than revealing such skeptical outlook. "I can't" is a self-fulfilling prophecy. This defeatist mentality leads to all sorts of mistakes that eventually compound into severe problems. Choosing this road intentionally, makes no sense, but how easily are you tempted to use any or all of these "anti" responses or declarations? Making errors are human stumbles, designed to test our ability to overcome adversity from time to time. Inviting them to happen, via negative reinforcement, is a matter in need of reversing focus in order to welcome a positive result.

"The enemy" delights hearing you say, "I can't." It's how control is kept over you. The good news is "the enemy" can't without your permission. The choice is yours. Breaking the habit of saying, "I can't" might be as difficult to conquer as smoking or chewing tobacco or any number of detriments. It takes a backbone, not a wishbone, to achieve merit. I hope you're not banking on the lottery. Inquisitive students frequently ask, "So, what did I do wrong?" This is another example of negative reinforcement. My reply is, "Nothing. What would you like to do better?"

"I can't stop slicing the ball. What should I do?"

"Don't slice it."

"But, I always slice my driver."

"Don't use your driver."

"But, I want to be able to."

"You already are."

"But, I can't stop slicing it."

"Then, you won't."

After a few more of these exchanges, the student usually becomes aware that at the root of the snafu is the conviction: "I can't."

"I'm having difficulty," implies help would be welcome. How can anyone accept or receive assistance after declaring, "I can't"? Anything's possible with a positive, certain, perspective. Instead of admitting and conceding failure (a favorite device of "the enemy") suppose stating, "With better understanding, I'm ready, willing and able, to do whatever is necessary." Now we can get somewhere. Too many people I listen to have pre-conceived notions that keep them stuck and unable to see the brighter side. A particular person had a propensity to "pull" the ball. "I just can't hit it straight." I could say, "You hit it straight. You just need to move the green over to where you aimed."

More than 90% of all cases "wanting" advice, seek solely mechanical solutions, when in fact, their announcements indicate an initial "thinking" malfunction requiring a mere attitude adjustment. The next time you "think" you've experienced a "bad shot", consider that it might only look bad from the perspective point where you are. By the time you reach where it is you'll discover a new "good shot" to negotiate. If you find yourself lost, or out of bounds, God only cares and probably not as much as you'd like. If you "think" it's important, I would recommend considering its irrelevance, *if* it matters more than, "What's for supper?" Now, doesn't that feel better? If you're really bothered (and I used to be), it will be obvious to others that a serious imbalance and naiveté of harmony exist. There's no reason to take years to wise up like I did. It's all about tuning in. Immediately is good.

I'm going to run a small list of typical, "I can't," excuses by. If any, or all, resemble familiar remarks, pay attention to how they sound (especially if you say it).

"It's too hard. I can't..."
"I can't stand it anymore."
"I can't sleep."
"I don't like vegetables."
"I can't lose weight."
"I can't hit my eight-iron."
"I can't break 100."
"I can't get along with my neighbor."
"I can't take it."
"I can't chip."
"I can't putt."
"I don't like this."
"I don't like that."
"Blah, blah, blah; I want my way; waah, waah, waah."

I've witnessed players missing hands, arms, and legs. None of them complained. They are true conquerors.

I'm convinced that the handicap system correlates directly to the number of excuses whiny players use to try to justify spiritual weakness. What folly of inconceivable nonsense. We're the only species that does this. Does this mean we're the smartest? I'm just asking. Handicap excuses have nothing to do with ability. I liken it to trying to gain wisdom from a computer. Hmmm... *If* you are a whiner, forgive me for not taking you seriously. There are more valuable times to spend.

Chapter IX

Goals and Dress Codes

Supposing goals are beneficial to have (depending on the motive), when they fail to serve the good of all by any means of selfish ambition, they become worthless at best and evil at worst. Therefore, it is a belief that the collective goal we all share is advancing the Kingdom of God (please read *Golf in the Kingdom* by Michael Murphy)—promoting His Glory by being the best we can be in honor of Him, since we are all His children. I know of no other way, but to discover this takes an ultimate amount of patience, trusting and faith. Anything short of this *total* commitment is deceit, resulting in failure to live up to one's very own greatness. That is really why, we are all here—isn't it?

I can recall an instance, when playing baseball in front of my father, who was watching from the stands. I had made spectacular catches before and expected to make them all, every time. This was one of my "goals". On this particular occasion, I was playing right field when the batter hit a deep fly ball toward right/center field. Instinctively, I knew the center fielder was too far away to get to it, so at the "crack of the bat" moment, I raced to my backhand side with all my might to run it down as it was carrying at least to the fence. Just as it was sailing above the top part, I timed my leap to meet it at the apex of flight with the webbing of my glove. In the flash of an instant, the ball ticked the end of my fingertips as I reached as far as I could stretch them. The ball abruptly made a carom to the ground for a home run. As the other team paused, then cheered, I felt jeered. Somehow it seemed I had made an error and let my teammates down. I surely let myself down.

I was so wrapped up in my selfish disappointment; I honestly can't remember the outcome of the game. I only know being upset that I had seemingly failed to make that play in our favor. Afterward, my dad, being consoling (we must have lost) and fatherly, wisely explained that I had given all of my best effort on the play. "What more could you ask for?"

"I should have caught it! I could have saved the game!" I exclaimed.

"Apparently," dad paused, calmly, "He deserved a home run even more." Interesting concept, wouldn't you agree? It surely spun my head.

Great results don't necessarily follow our wishes or plans. If you "think" God doesn't have a sense of humor, go ahead and set your goals. However, His plans always work better than ours. Working together is the answer, and the key. It is guaranteed. I no longer get disappointed. Before I learned "going with the flow", I always tried to make the flow go my way. Then I was constantly disappointed… That was idiotic. I once was oblivious to the significance of how I dressed. I wanted to be "cool" and look the part. I wanted my hair long; I wanted to wear tight jeans; I wanted to "show off" for the girls. I imagine this is all part of puberty, but there eventually comes a time for all of us to grow up. "Flashy", being the opposite of "sloppy", can actually appear more "clownish". A suggestion that I learned is to clothe in a dignified and cleanly manner. Being this way commands respect, but taking another step further is to respect all others for the way they appear. It is an obligation to look our best. Take joy in it and always remember before going out in public—most importantly, wear your smile!

How you dress is what you attract. It's that "birds of a feather flock together" thing. If you choose to dress in a slovenly, disrespectful attitude, it's simple to figure out who you'll be hanging out with. It's that "misery loves company" thing. If you need to get over yourself, just do it. The company you choose to keep is up to you. Life is your blessing. You can be grateful and giving thanks just by wearing a sincere smile. You'll be amazed at what happens. God is goodness. Happiness resides with Him. The "code" is not a secret. Wouldn't you rather get in agreement? Life goes better!

Chapter X

Gambling & Competition (The "Macho" Addiction)

Contrary to popular belief, golf is not a competition. Gambling on who is better than whom is a relentless effort in futility. Haven't you experienced resentment or a desire to get even? Cain did. It's difficult to understand the claim that gambling's fun. "Fast Eddie" (the "hot shot" pool player) got his fingers broken and he was one of the best. Many who have taken too much have gone missing. Indulging in this activity (and most everyone has, including me), doesn't begin to compare with the satisfaction and contentment of knowing each of us are equal in our Heavenly Father's eyes. Pleasing to Him when we give our best under any circumstance is not anything to be judged humanly. The realization that we're all masterpieces, created differently, would seem to change minds on this matter.

Golf is not a conquest over anybody, either. Thinking so is shameful. Who might you be "trying" to be better than? Toughness is not based on how many pounds can be bench pressed or on the size of tires a pick-up truck has. Nope, it's not even a contest. Trying to make it such is silly and misses the point. After completing my training course in 1978, I took the remainder of my vacation time to spend in Las Vegas. I was young, brash and too overconfident. Upon noticing this, a man I met as a stranger and I, set out to play a round of golf together. He asked my handicap and not knowing any better at that time I told him a bit of the experience I'd just had and that prior to it, a two was assigned. I asked him his, to which, he declared himself a fifteen. Being as dumb as a stick and gullible, I naively agreed to give five strokes per side. What a sucker set up I fell for! Well, to say the least, I learned my lesson. Never again!

Now, when approached by gamblers, I enjoy announcing, "I'm not interested in your money and I'm surely not giving you mine." It doesn't make any difference, even if it's only a nickel. I'm not here to have to prove anything to anybody. I just need to be obedient to God and grateful for all His blessings, of which there are so many. I was actually pleased to turn 50 several years ago. I no longer required pursuing the egotistic notion that I needed to shoot from the furthest tees back, *anymore*. This relates to the "macho" addiction. The affliction infects way too many men, but even some women are not immune. Here's another analogy: suppose you're having a 65th birthday. This is the standard acceptable age for becoming a senior of society. The golf *Tour* places the number at 50, whereas a "super" senior, need only be 60 years old. Okay now, your big opportunity has arrived, but instead of taking it (as a gift), you choose to still hit from the back tees.

"Sir, would you like the senior discount, today?"

"Nope. I prefer to pay the full price. I want you to charge me more.

This is how much sense is made by doing this. That's what "ego" does to people. Occasionally I'm told, "You should be playing from the back tees."

My response is, "When I get too good to be playing from up here, I'll move back (like that's ever going to happen). I'm not 30 anymore."

Almost all of the people I watch who appear over-aged and/or under-qualified try to play "over their heads" this way.

Seldom do they leave the parking lot smiling and a good many of them go off "half-tanked" in sorrow, reflecting upon what went wrong before the 19th hole. One gent we used to play with a few years back was then in his earlier 60s. We noticed he was easily intimidated. While my other friends and I would choose to play the senior tees, this man insisted on punishing himself from the younger men's tees (he was definitely disgruntled with the *extra* effort). When asked, "Why?" he said, "My wife makes me." At that time, his wife was one of the better players in the women's club. We knew she regularly beat up on this poor guy.

"She makes you?! What are you, a wuss? Real men accept their fallacies. Be a man and come play up here with us." Reluctantly, at first, he did. His perspective was altered, but he still felt guilty for some odd reason. In learning to understand this principle at school, each student was given these options to choose from:

1. Take your distance off the tee and the result if you were in the rough.
2. Mark your distance if you were out of bounds and re-tee with a two stroke penalty.
3. Consider your over-aggressiveness by sacrificing 30 yards and put your ball in the middle of the fairway.

This is an exceptional means to realize that golf was never designed to be a hitting contest. Oh sure, they have those, but that's not what the game is all about.

My high school buddy and I, as well as our teammates, were at a distinct disadvantage compared with the hoity-toity schools. We had to match-up with the country club kids whose parents afforded them the most privileged environments (there is nothing wrong with that—other than being looked down at). We, on the other hand, had a nice guy for our coach, who couldn't break 50 for nine holes. In an attempt to square the odds a little more evenly, when it was our home course advantage, my pal and I would sneak on to the playing field the night before a match and move up all the tee markers. There was a quite a bit of *"buzz"* about it. I don't know if it made much difference actually, but we were better prepared. At least we had a fair chance and more fun, while the other guys griped and overshot the greens more often.

Throughout history, man has been "trying" to beat man. They spit and snort and drink and cuss and frown a lot—carrying on their rituals. I have been "thinking" and "trying" to come up with any good reason to justify competition in the first place. I have concluded (thank God), that I don't have to since I didn't create it, anyway. Whew, that's a load off my mind. I mention a few examples, perhaps a bit "tongue in cheek" for your consideration... What is the good purpose for rioting over a soccer game? Uh... doesn't this, kind of, tend to lead to war? What is proven if a muscle is torn during weight-lifting? Doesn't anybody get dizzy watching cars race in a circle? Who thinks their numbers are really going to be chosen when the chances against that happening are about 250 million to your one? There must be a point, somewhere. Well, I suppose it can all just be sportingly good fun. Goliath thought so. David didn't. The principle is the same whether today or long ago.

Al Capone was idolized and feared by many for his toughness and brutality. How ironic that in this monster's inevitable demise, V.D. took him down. Even all the negative energy he wasted for evil purposes was no match for Adolf. This embodiment of Satan took the most cowardly exit. Anyone has the right to *doubt* or *deny*. If we all thought that way, consider how miniscule it would make our relevance. That would be worse than sad. Gracefully and mercifully, God's infinite wisdom and positive power rules forever, over all. Goodness always triumphs!

Chapter XI

Cheating & Electronic Dishonesty

Golf is not a game for gizmos (unless you are Rodney Dangerfield in *Caddy Shack*—the premier cheater). Like too many who choose to look for the easy way out, cheating only serves to verify an unwillingness to stand up to adversity. This means that when real challenges need to be confronted, the courage required to do so isn't there. This is why cheaters *always* end up the losers. I previously felt compelled to have to win, when scoring and competing seemed to matter. I was slow to discover that it doesn't. The side effect became an immersion in self-doubt and condemnation. I thought I hated golf, but was actually obsessed with the common addiction of "trying" to beat yesterday's score. I was willing to "try" almost any means to do so.

At about age 55, a divine intervention came to me in the form of a wonderful friend who understood this problem and helped me overcome my affliction. I was mentored into learning that scoring is actually meaningless and corrupt in its application, which is *judgmental comparison*. When the realization finally struck the right chord, I was held captive no more. I became free to enjoy God's gift to me. It's just that simple. You can do it, too. On the contrary, as long as the temptation to compare is entrenched, jealousy, envy and covetous behavior will continue to prevail, through any means of unfair practice—cheating. Many golf aficionados focus on a handful of their televised favorites. They measure their scores, rate and judge with discrimination and carry on with artificially hierarchic rankings, ad-nauseam.

I had the privilege of following Sam Snead when he was playing as a "super senior". I don't know if he was completely blind in one eye or severely limited in sight. He was simply an amazing player and a joy to watch. His skill level and creativity were unparalleled. His uniqueness was on display when he designed his own croquet style putter, which he used very effectively by playing the ball directly facing forward from the middle of his stance and striking it thus in mallet fashion. At the time, the powers in charge deemed this practice illegal. They may have decided that since Sam was already too good to begin with, he must be gaining an even further unfair advantage. Ah yes, the "rules of competition" committee strikes again. He was made to turn sideways, in order to force conformity.

Do you remember a fellow, who for a brief while on *The Tour*, played on a badly crippled leg and needed cart assistance to alleviate some of his pain? Of course, this wasn't fair to many of the other players that he should be allowed to ride. Instead of letting anyone ride who needed or wanted to or just quit complaining, this courageous man was made to suffer and walk. This is as if you were to say to Grandma, "It's too bad you're limping, but if you don't start walking normally, you can't have a wheelchair." Sam Snead's putting stroke was lost afterward and the rest of us were deprived, as well. There must be standards, after all. As guidelines must be required in any competitive endeavor, contradictions abound, while the "odds makers" lick their chops. In vain attempts to gain unfair advantage (cheat), there have been some disgusting examples of "doping", "steroid abuse" and "fixing", just to name a few. When money and/or pride are at stake, is it any wonder, what greed and temptation does?

As golf balls evolved from leather-stitched "featheries" to "wound cores" to "solid centers," clubs went from wooden shaft and head, to graphite, titanium and beyond. Club heads used to be limited in size, but we know the "cat got let out of the bag" on that one. Drivers and putters have reached ridiculously proportionate levels, both in design and cost. I would be questioned as to the legality of my 50-inch driver. Excuse me, by whose rules? Please, don't make me laugh. Okay, make me laugh. What would anyone care if it were 60 inches long? I use my standards and I'm mainly playing for exhibition and glee, anyway. Golf is pure in its nature. Modifications and rule additions, can serve as a means to accommodate more elaborate ways of cheating. It is kind of like making new laws. Each time another one is written and enacted, we *tend* (but not always) to lose a little bit more of our freedom.

The "new-fangled" electronic devices being introduced on a near daily basis are described by at least one "master-pro" as, "Helpful aids to make the game more fun." Really?! If I'm too lazy to figure things out with my God given-gift (a brain—which was built better, guaranteed for life and costs less), then I might as well chop my head off and sew a button on. Now *that's* something to "think" about. Oh yeah, I can't; I don't have a head. When somebody yells, "Hey, button head!" I won't be able to hear, either. Oh…Never mind. I don't aim to stir up any more controversy. Only God knows the answers. As for us, respect for our differences would seem prudent. God does love us all.

Chapter XII

The Driving Range

There is no connection between the driving range and the course, itself. No amount of practice shots can prepare a person to be cast out into the open. There's a huge difference between pseudo and real. Practicing simulations is equivalent to pretending to pay bills with fake money. Real situations demand a willingness to pay attention to the task at hand. Mistakes can't be overcome unless they are conquered in real time. Errors on the driving range reinforce the notion that it's okay, because it's not for real. The compromised attitude is real and the will suffers for it.

"Well, I'm working on my swing."

"I need to warm up, before I play."

Alright; how long does the plan to be a beginner take? Instead, here's a recommendation that has served me well for many years: Wake up slowly and deliberately. Take your time and give thanks for being blessed to live another day! Enjoy every moment everywhere you go before you arrive. Then, when you get there, relax and stretch out any tenseness at the first tee. You are ready! That's all there is to it. I notice most of the same people where I play practice day after day the exact same swings over and over and over and over again and again and again! How can their realms ever expand? Maybe they don't want them to. Perhaps they don't know it's possible. They could even be afraid. Why though, would anyone not want to increase his or her potential beyond the "practice" of constantly being and staying the same?

The bottom line is there is no substitution for actual performing. There are many things that can be practiced. Music comes to mind. Teams rehearse plays, etc. I'm sure many examples can be devised. I believe this is where skiing and golf are prime exceptions, where one chance at the moment is all you get. Wouldn't it make certain sense to be in the moment more often, to experience joy and wonderment, in a plethora of real situations, gaining knowledge and growing more confident all the while? There are no consequences on the driving range (unless maybe you hit the person next to you). Let's suppose, you pay about five dollars for a bucket of around 60 balls; because it's called a driving range, I guess for many, the assumption is to use the driver predominately. Usually, approximately two thirds of the amount of balls dispensed is used up with this one club. As a result, shots are scattered short, long, left and right. Very little accomplishment is made, other than a waste of energy. This may be a way to blow off steam after work. I don't know about you, but after eight hours of work, I'm really tired.

This appears to be more of an exercise in futility and frustration, above anything else. All you've done is made a mess for somebody getting paid to clean it up. Are you going to be comfortable with that? My intent is not to criticize effort. I do propose to challenge irrational behavior by introducing different perspectives in order to receive positive, productive and meaningful results. It's a conviction to lead a purposeful life. We're all eventually going to have to answer for ours by giving a personal account anyway. I've wasted enough time already. How about you? It's never too late to get started. I hope you're still with me. As **Red Green** puts it, "Remember, I'm pulling for you. We're all in this together." As the band **Kansas** sings it, "We can't escape the times we live in." If only one thing is to be learned from the movie ***Tin Cup***, it's that "style" supersedes any score far more effectively, importantly and entertainingly (save for maybe below 30 for nine holes and less than 60 for eighteen although I believe that either one case or the other, or both, would first come under the category of "style", anyway).

An exemplary incident occurred recently as I was playing a casual Sunday afternoon nine holes with a very dear friend. The two of us started off well, making pars and birdies. By the fourth hole (a par five, with a six foot wide water ditch, crossing about two thirds the distance from tee to green), I sat about 50 yards short of the hazard—my companion nearly 90, with our first shots each in the middle of the fairway. My partner, shooting from furthest away, sent a low, scalding liner at ground level that struck my ball directly, propelling it at a high rate of speed straight forward toward the water hazard, as his careened sideways left. We watched, in hilarious bewilderment, while my ball ran a good 50 yards (not feet) climbed the front side bank and came to rest—perched on the edge. After the laughter subsided (which took several minutes to "catch our breaths"), we considered ignoring the "rules committee" to play on (for rules freaks, my ball was returned to its original position). We had witnessed a record ricochet. What else mattered?

I don't remember my score for that day, but I'll always remember that shot! The occurrence could never have become history had we just spent our time at the driving range, practicing that most improbable event.

Where was ESPN?

Another most memorable moment happened on the eleventh hole—a par three, when a different friend and I were being observed by a former player, standing by his parked vehicle, viewing from an open spot on a hill nearby. He could see as we teed off simultaneously side by side. When our shots "crisscrossed" in midair (his, with a left to right fade, mine, with a right to left draw), bounce at virtually the same point and moment, then both roll up and stop at "tap-in" close birdie range, our buddy, in exasperated shock, replied, "Show-offs!" He disgustedly shook his head, got in his car and drove away. His dog didn't seem to mind. How much fun was that? We laughed tears and howled uncontrollably, until we collapsed to the ground in exhaustion—our guts hurting and cramping, while neither of us particularly cared whether we died at that moment. That's how much fun we have! It's so simple. Give it a chance. Just go play!

Chapter XIII

Public Vs. Private

About the same time I decided to turn professional, another acquaintance I knew from a different high school, did the same, both independently. He came from a well-known golfing family, noted for more than a couple of generations as great players with top notch abilities. His caliber was up there amongst at least the best in our State (I have lived in several and was born in Massachusetts. I won't mention which one we were from at that time. You may soon understand why). He and I once discussed similarities in reasoning over choosing "independence" rather than becoming "affiliated." However, this was not a popular perspective and not always received or respected well (and sometimes not at all—frowned on, in other words) by others... if you can catch my drift.

My last year (1978) as an amateur, I played in my State's open championship. The following year, I applied as a pro, but was denied entry. I won't expound here, but let my continuance shift attention to my colleague. Within a couple of years afterward (I had dismissed appealing), my cohort was facing the same discriminatory situation. What he did next was brilliant... Neighboring Wyoming accepted his entry enthusiastically. When he won their State Open that year, the news spread through the newspapers like wildfire and hit home hard. Can you picture the red faces? He was quite the "talk of the town"—a local hero. He certainly had my applause.

What do you suppose this has to do with public versus private? Let me use my favorite example for comparison. When the movie ***Animal House*** arguably (I suppose) became the number one favorite comedy of all time, it was initially presumed that the "Deltas" were the animals. The "Omegas" were assuming themselves to be the self-righteous role-model majority. We know how that turned out. I believe we can mostly understand that appearances often and usually wind up being opposite to reality. Interestingly, this *classic* has withstood the test of time, continuing to be a smash hit forever. "Publicly" and "privately" I believe, are best separated by bathroom or bedroom doors. "Public" and "private" on the other hand, imply entirely different meanings. Is it any wonder that people with bi-polar disorders, face tremendous difficulties?

It is my conviction—I'm not exaggerating to say—that "public" translates to "total openness". It should not be confined to stipulations. In other words, public, means free, as in freedom and/or "open" (key word). Contrastingly, "private" is the upside down version ("closed"). When there are "private" meetings, "private" properties, "private" clubs, "private" memberships, "private" associations, or "private" anything, it infers everything has to be hidden, kept secret or kept closed. It's discriminatory. Who or what, aren't they willing to accept? If you are looking from the outside and are not invited in, then you are putting yourself in Joseph and Mary's position. Do you like it? Would you like to treat other people that way?

What's the fear here?

Is it not exposure?

What's being *revealed* is the *truth*. Ooh... how bad is that? It is good. It is Godly. We don't need to have "private" relationships with Him. Going "privately" about it may be more politely discretionary. I don't believe He enjoys us being pious towards

Him. It serves Him just as well to be open ("public" about it) and honest, continuously, now and forevermore. He loves *all* of us and wants us to love Him, simply and personally, without being afraid to be "open" about it.

Chapter XIV

Costs A. Personal (Commitment) B. Prices (Economic)

Commitment is nothing short of total. It's not one third, one half, or even three quarters. Its synonym, dedication, is a full time job—24/7. Whether you're an Oakland Raider fan or not, their motto is, "Committed to Excellence." This isn't just a mere slogan. This is a way of life. It's what God calls us all to be. There is no failure. There may be temporary setbacks but, it's all a matter of perspective. Achievement is attained through relentless striving to overcome obstacles. There will always be stumbling blocks on life's trek. Warriors face onslaughts of challenges on a continuous basis. They might not win all battles (with or without weapons), but they get up and get going again. Pity parties are for quitters (non-committers).

"Release the full you." —Joel Osteen

Holding back commitment is anally retentive and we all know how painful that can be. Laxatives won't solve the problem (although they might offer temporary relief). We need full commitment in order to break through any and all problems. Have faith and be determined to come out of your cocoon. There is an abundance of good that can chase any evil but, no one can be successful by just "dipping their toes in the water". Totally immerse yourself and be cleansed. There's no need to be combative and/or belligerent about it, as I had to learn. God is kind and merciful. He is the "lifter" of us *all*. He doesn't step all over us. He allows us our "free will". When we decide, in defiance, to go our own way is when we fall all over ourselves. Be committed to give your best under all circumstances. Never mind your own expectations or doing things to "try" to impress other people. God gave you your strengths and He knows your weaknesses. Trust Him to know the best way. Stop worrying. Just commit to it!

We don't have a spending problem in this country. God can afford anything we need. What we do have is a cost problem. Prices are the difficulty. There's always going to be a "better mouse trap" to be made for a lower cost. That's just a first example. Where we've gotten off on the wrong track, is by taking the backward approach, of making everything more expensive. Greed hurts everybody. Should a round of golf really cost 50 dollars, to hundreds or even thousands? Come on… I used to pay $2.75 to play 18 holes (yes, in my lifetime). I remember when my dad was living; he loved the show **The Price Is Right** with Bob Barker. Automobiles then had been valued moderately, in the $3,000 to $6,000 range, for a good quality, American built car, as I recollected.

On this particular show I once watched with him was a standard brand, certain model type, to guess a figure on. I gave it a stab at approximately, $4,800. Before the actual cost was revealed, the moderator gave a lengthy description of the car and all its luxurious features while the show models smiled and danced all around it. The surprise moment had arrived to reveal the expense. When it was announced the word "worth" caught my attention. I had underbid by nearly $4,000! My instinctive reaction was "What the h—?" It might *cost* that much, but it surely was not *worth* that much to me. Enough people must have bought it however, because prices have kept going higher!

I was working in those days for $3.86 per hour (and that was "journey-man's" pay that I had to work two years to earn). I could afford anything I needed. My point is look at what we've done to ourselves in just 35 years. Strikes for higher wages and bigger benefits were common and frequent in those times. I remember hearing the argument from management's point of view, that if wages had to be increased, then prices on everything would have to go up, as well. This happened, of course. As many of us can recall the gas wars—a gallon could be purchased for 19 cents. The cost of a small box of "animal crackers" was about the same. Just the other day I was in a convenience store and happened to notice the same item was more than three dollars. What?! I could go on... I believe you get the picture.

Chapter XV

Golf's Current Culture

I want to be careful here, but I need to be truthful. A lot of the problems many complain about today are reflective in golf's current culture. Now, this isn't to say that a lot of positive doesn't exist (it does) because it all depends on how we choose to look at the matter. There is too much "pride and prejudice". (I know there's a good book with that title, by the way. Maybe we should read it (again)). My father, Theodore Ward, was a wonderful man and dad. It comes as a surprise to me and perhaps would to him also, that in his passing, he became so popular. His initials, *"T.W."*, on hats all around are quite the tribute. Being considered an icon or regarding himself as such is sinful, naturally (everybody should know that). If he had been a prideful man he would have worn one himself. I liked him better that he wasn't and he didn't respectively and respectfully (pun intended).

While treating my mother with love, adoration and faithfulness, he was respectful of all races, colors and creeds. He was a modest, humble man—honest by every measure and, although he was by no means perfect and definitely not wealthy, his 87-year life was dedicated and devoted to principle, truth and goodwill toward all. He was considered a very rich man and his father shook hands with Abraham Lincoln! One thing he wasn't, was a golf enthusiast, although we shared moments of enjoyment watching Nicklaus, Trevino, Player, Watson, Rodriguez, Sifford, Peete, Kite, Crenshaw, Floyd, Barber, Boros, Casper, Aoki, Ballesteros, Green, Palmer and many exceptional others, for their particularly unique styles. They all shared greatness in their own different ways and we could tell them apart. Also, there were the ladies who were   every bit as good as the men (but, unfortunately and unfairly far less compensated).   Stars such as Alcott, Berg, Bradley, Carner, Daniel, Davies, Haynie, Inkster, King, Little, Lopez, Mallon, Okamoto, Pak, Palmer, Rankin, Rawls, Sheehan, Stacy, Sorenstam, Webb, Whitworth, Wright and of course Jan Stephenson (who might have been even more famous for sending men to their chiropractors with "whiplash"), amongst several more "greats", would even attract Mom to the living room.

After the "Golden Bear" won the Masters in 1986, it seemed a "new wave" of players was ushered in to change the face of the game (as well as the rules). Technology increased and resources (like persimmon wood) decreased. The emphasis on distance and robotics exploded. Video lessons and fad aids were all the rage. Costs were becoming more and more prohibitive for many, while fashions went crazy as well. "Yuppies" entered the picture and the game spread to the suburbs. This didn't seem such a bad thing however, as more and more corporations were developing bigger, better and more extravagant courses. Affordability mainly depended upon "keeping up", culturally speaking. Then there came a saturation point and recession. Revenues dipped and as a result of lost income, the common retribution to the public was to keep raising prices. This was—and still is—opulently outrageous! Where's Robin Hood when we need him?

Being your own sponsor (unless you were extremely wealthy), would become a virtual impossibility. Therefore, sponsors ultimately took over the game. It didn't just happen to golf. I can remember general admission to a baseball game was only a couple of bucks. The best (box) seats could be purchased for maybe $5 or $6. Football games might have let you in for maybe $8, for starters. Heck, I even recall spending a huge amount of allowance ($6.60), to see The Beatles in 1964 at Red Rocks Amphitheater. What happened? Was this Progress? When I turn on the television and see virtually every player on *The Tour* now wearing a logo hat, a different logo shirt, ads on their pants, shoes, gloves, bags, balls, clubs, and everything else I may have left out, I wonder what's real about that person. I don't have the stomach to be remotely interested anymore. I just turn it off. At least they can't kill the memories.

Chapter XVI

Comedy / Drama

The choice is perfectly clear. Do I want to be entrapped, self-serious, judgmental, hateful, fearful, full of trepidation, suspicious, prejudiced, bigoted, homophobic, incessantly pessimistic, totally freaked out and controlled by persistent misery and lies ("Remind you of anyone?" —Craig Ferguson)? As tempting as that all sounds, I would rather be happy, a bit aloof, loving, caring, at peace, raring-to-go, trusting, straight forward, accepting, giving, tolerant, understanding, compassionate, empathetic, self-controlled, gentle, kind, considerate, eternally optimistic and in tune with all things (*All Creatures Great and Small*—another terrific book). Nearing conclusion, I would like to extrapolate on a few whimsical comparisons of opposite, peculiar behavior. My hope is we'll all find fun in our flaws. There are a couple of characters, you've undoubtedly met, but perhaps didn't recognize or know their names.

It's difficult to know where to start to describe "LOU-E", but I'll give it a whirl. He, she or it (although I believe it's probably a cross between he and it), became apparent several years ago, when I was mentored to know how to be cognizant and deal with the disguises. One thing known for certain is that, "LOU-E" is the "Master of Disaster", the "King of Chaos" and the "Dean of Deception" all rolled into one. Shape changing and time travel is no bounds, for this impish creature to intrude, adding trickery and treachery to your daily activities. Danger is also a distinct possibility, unless you can protect yourself by turning the tables on this impetus gremlin. Getting angry invites "LOU-E" to ratchet up the annoyances, specifically and individually crafted, that pertain to "getting your goat". I've discovered "LOU-E" doesn't know how to react when spotted.

When eye contact is made is when the really good fun starts. That "blank" stare is often the giveaway. If you can pick him/her/it out of a crowd or a herd or a flock, or a swarm, or just anything that seems out of place ("LOU-E" could be disguised as anything as small as a gnat, to something as big as "The Sky (is Falling)" —Chicken Little), you should note either the fake fur or possibly plastic-looking feathers or maybe a barely visible propeller on the top of the head or end of the nose (you might really have to squint to see it). Do you notice that spider walking across your target line? You just *think* it's a spider— "LOU-E". Don't squash it! You will find out something's definitely going on. Let it go. It was put there for a reason. "LOU-E" is not to be denied the ability to throw you off your game. Whether you accept the existence or not, doesn't make any difference.

The best way I have found to at least keep "LOU-E" at bay is to never take your eye off the ball (both literally and figuratively). You might think you're in bounds, but in that brief moment of a half instant when you weren't paying attention, your ball could be kicked out of bounds. Oh, "LOU-E" can be quick, also (warp speed). You can learn to have outstandingly funny experiences (at "LOU-E's" expense) only if you can tolerate the unlimited sense of humor on display and see it for what it is worth. You can also try to fight it (like the wind, it's a losing proposition). Sinners are really easy. Macho pretenders are favorite targets. Now, don't tell anybody this, but I have an evil twin, that even my parents didn't know about, named "Bill". "Bill" likes to invite himself along wherever I go and unwittingly create nuisances. He borrows my clubs, hits wildly erroneous shots all over the place and then makes me go after them. He plays with the authority of awfulness.

He and "LOU-E" are close cousins. As relatives, they are extremely chummy. I've done my best to throw him off, but I've found the most efficient way to lose him, is by doing "the spin" combined with "the chant". In dire situations of abounding lousy shots, "the spin" is a method used to confuse and in turn, shake free the mixed thought patterns. It's the most efficient way to cure playing like a dufus. Two trips around the club handle (with head attached) as fast as you can go then, reversing direction and doing it again, has quite the dizzying effect. By shaking the cobwebs out of the brain, this can remedy the immediate problem. However, to be sure, it's recommended that in severe cases of "boneheaditis", adding an ancient tribal war dance cry in rapid succession of "Hi-how-are-ya", repeatedly over and over, will definitely fix your troubles. It works remarkably well. A really good laugh always beats anger.

Okay, so "Bill" is really my alter-ego. Actually, he is my ego. He still creeps around occasionally. I have to stay focused. "Remind you of anyone?" If you remain a gambler who likes to compete and take yourself seriously (like all drama kings and queens do), just know from here on that the outcome has already been "manipulated". Watchful eyes are upon you. Now, if you see a suspicious looking rabbit, with a "Velcro" cotton ball for a tail, check to see if there's a "wind-up" key underneath (if you can get close enough) and a wink to go with it. Then, you'll know you've been had. Laughter heals the sick and wounded. Lighten up. Otherwise, I guess your option would be, to stay stupidly upset and blame the world ("Remind you of anyone?"). Bagger Vance said, "Why don't you just hook it to hell and gone? Put yourself out of your misery. That way, you'll be so far out of the match, we can just relax and enjoy ourselves, the rest of the way..."

What are you waiting for? "Are you sure that you're not sure?" —Jacinto Iniguez

Conclusion

A Summary of What Golf Is

There is nothing you can hide. All your weaknesses; all your strengths are known. God reveals them completely. You bear no shield. No gun can protect you. You are naked in this world. You do possess, one instrument—a sword (club, if you will). That's all. Golf is not a joke. It is a riddle. It surely fooled me for the longest time and then, I got it.

1. Golf is an individual journey of the soul.
2. Golf is a walk with God.
3. Golf is the: **G**ame **O**f **L**ife, **F**ool.

Metaphorically, the ball is your spirit. Let it soar!

CPSIA information can be obtained at www.ICGtesting.com
Printed in the USA
LVOW05s0005230114

370544LV00001B/2/P